Mapping American History
A Guide for Beginning Students

GERALD A. DANZER
University of Illinois at Chicago

HarperCollins*Publishers*

Executive Editor: Bruce Borland
Developmental Editor: Rebecca W. Strehlow
Project Coordination: Lucy Lesiak Design, Inc.
Cover Design: Lucy Lesiak Design, Inc.
Text Design: Lucy Lesiak Design, Inc.
Photo Research: Judy Ladendorf
Cartographer: Paul Yatabe. Maps produced by
      Mapping Specialists, Inc.
Production: Michael Weinstein
Compositor: Lucy Lesiak Design, Inc.
Printer and Binder: Malloy Lithographing, Inc.
Cover Printer: Malloy Lithographing, Inc.

ACKNOWLEDGMENTS

Topic	Credit
5	Armin K. Lobeck
10	The New York Historical Society, New York City
13	Library of Congress
14, 26	Paullin
19	Historic Urban Plans
21	Adapted from Robert D. Mitchell and Paul A. Graves, eds., *North America* (Totowa, NJ: Rowman & Littlefield, 1987), p. 301
22	The Library, University of Illinois Chicago
25	Courtesy Sear, Robuck and Co.
29	From *An Atlas of Soviet Affairs* © 1965, Text by Robert N. Taafe, Map by Robert C. Kingsbury. Reprinted by permission of Henry Holt and Company.
31	Stanley Brunn, *Geography and Politics in America,* HarperCollins*Publishers,* 1974
32	J. F. Rooney, Dept. of Geography, Oklahoma State University

Cover: L'Enfant's Plan for the National Capitol,
Library of Congress

Mapping American History:
A Guide for Beginning Students

Copyright © 1991 by HarperCollins Publishers Inc.

ISBN 0-673-53768-4

90 91 92 93   9 8 7 6 5 4 3 2 1

CONTENTS

APPENDIXES
Answers
Extra World Maps (3)
Blank Timelines
Key to Textbooks

INTRODUCTION

The three essential ingredients of history are people, place, and time. To be good students of the past, and to effectively operate in the present, we must be familiar with each of these basic dimensions.

People come first, as individuals to be sure, but more importantly in history's eyes, as members of groups and societies. Clio, the muse of history, centers her attention on the experiences of particular groups of people, and she usually employs a story format to tell something about a particular human adventure. Her narratives make suggestions about the meaning and purpose of life by precept, by example, by their structure, and by the way the story is told. Some forms of historical presentation, including textbooks, are often very explicit in their analysis, listing causes and results, explaining the importance of events, or clearly suggesting the meaning of the past for the present. These interpretative features distinguish a historical account from a chronicle, the listing of events in chronological order without the connecting tissue of a narrative or the explicit commentary of a textbook or monograph.

At the college level a history course opens up new worlds for students as they perceive, often for the first time, the depth and richness of the subject. In the course of your study, you will begin to feel the powerful pull of Clio's charms, discovering history as a way of looking at life and the human condition while exploring its fascinating range of interpretative possibilities. History may present difficulties as well. Foremost among these is a sense of frustration.

Beginning students are often overwhelmed by the immensity of the past. How can one keep everything straight? Here is where the other two basic ingredients of history prove their value.

Time and space provide a matrix for locating people and their events so that everything can be kept in order. Dates and places serve as reference points for the immense amount of information found in your textbook.

Mapping American History is designed to help you put things in order so that your study of the past can move quickly to the fascinating level that wrestles with meaning and significance. This book is partly a handbook, partly a laboratory manual, and partly a study guide. It focuses on places and the spatial context of America's story. Maps are the usual mode of presentation, although timelines appear at regular intervals as a kind of map for temporal affairs.

Mapping American History expects you to do the job. It asks you to complete the maps and to work out the temporal sequences. It is hoped that you will make discoveries along the way, and that the discipline of systematically going through each topic will help you put things together into a meaningful synthesis. Then, as you break into the clear with a thrill of new insight, don't be afraid to crack a smile of satisfaction or to exclaim: "I see— that's how this stuff fits together!"

Several features occur regularly in this manual. "Places" deals with basic geographical data you will record on an outline map. "Working with Space" leads onward to an understanding of the basic spatial factors present in the activity. "Working with Time" provides a chronological context for your study, using both the diachronic and the synchronic functions of temporal order. The "Extensions" provide an opportunity for you to do a variety of writing projects. In some ways they are the culmination of each lesson.

Where short answers are called for, an answer key is provided in the appendix. However, recording answers is not really at the heart of the process. The lessons focus on developing skills of observation, on analyzing documents, and on bringing various facts or events together in a device that suggests connections between them.

Our goal is to eventually tie the major blocks of time and space together so that you will have a sense of American history as a whole. Then you will be in a position to control the textbook and to use this mastery as a springboard to the real purpose of studying the past: understanding who we are, knowing where we came from, and deciding where we want to go from here. As on any journey, it is best to have a map in your head as well as a map in your hand. *Mapping American History* is now something for your hand, but its goal is to give you the mental map as well. Bon voyage!

Gerald A. Danzer

Mapping American History
A Guide for Beginning Students

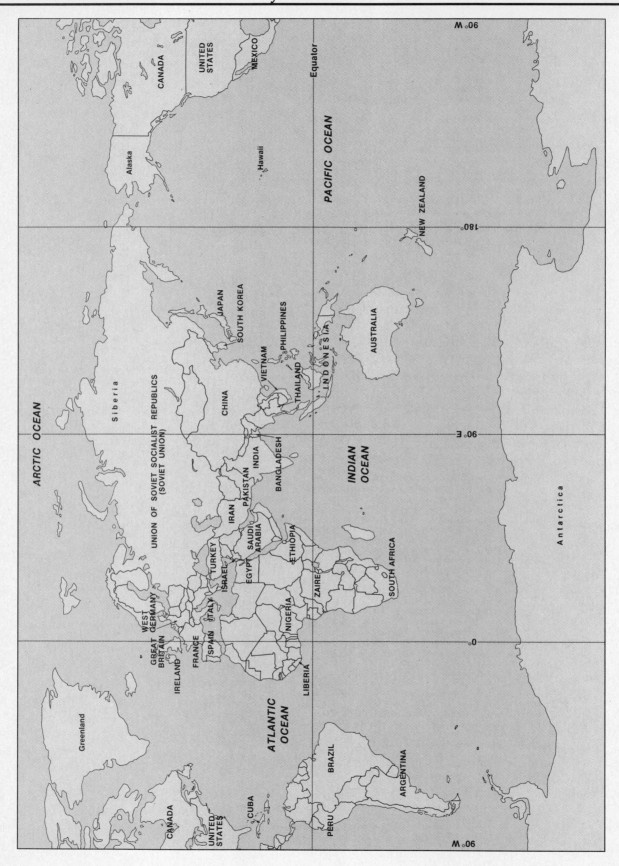

TOPIC 1
A World Context for American History: Places

BACKGROUND

Every conception of American history begins and ends with a global context. This is true in cartography as well as historiography. From the beginning American historians had to go elsewhere to begin and to end their narratives. George Bancroft, often called the most nationalistic of the major American historians, used the first line of his ten–volume narrative to declare that the United States was part of a "great political system, embracing all the civilized nations of the earth."

Bancroft's world view, however was centered in northwestern Europe. American history was thus an extension of the Old World story, a development that carried the promise of a new world, a new age, and a new humanity, but nevertheless remained part and parcel of the history of Western civilization.

The themes of America's world roots and its global mission became common assumptions on which the accounts of national history were based. A world map appropriate for American history thus centered on the Atlantic Ocean to emphasize the connection between Western Europe and the Americas.

The first Americans, however, who came thousands of years earlier, reached North America by a Pacific gateway. By the 1980s, the Asian connection had become so important to the United States that pundits hailed a new "Pacific Century" in American history. An appropriate world context map, in their view, would be one centered on the Pacific Rim with Hawaii in the center.

The map presented here is a compromise between these two orientations. Rather than emphasize an Atlantic or a Pacific connection it tries to do both. This map has a challenging look to it. Students of American history will be forced to look both east and west. The Old World is unified and the New World is seen as an outer belt of land relating to Europe, Africa, and Asia.

PLACES

1. The four oceans according to tradition are labeled on the map. Be sure you can locate them. Notice that there is really only one "World Ocean." Label it on the map in such a way so the name "World Ocean" extends from the Atlantic across the Indian Ocean to the Pacific.

2. Of the continents, only Antarctica is named. Label North America, South America, Africa, Europe, and Asia.

3. Native American Indians are thought to have come to the continent by way of the Bering Strait or a broad expanse of land connecting Asia and North America during the Ice Age. This region is often called Beringia. Label it on the map.

4. All Americans at some time in the past came from a place in the Old World. Place an "X" on a spot in Europe, Africa, or Asia you might consider your ancestral home.

5. Note how South America is situated farther east than North America. The entire southern continent lies to the east of Tampa, Florida.

A GLOBAL QUIZ (True or False)

_____ 1. China is located on the Indian Ocean.

_____ 2. The equator crosses Africa.

_____ 3. Part of Europe lies west of the Prime Meridian.

_____ 4. South America is the continent closest to Antarctica.

_____ 5. Of all the continents, Europe is the one most broken up by indentations of the world ocean and its seas.

_____ 6. Hawaii is the U.S. state closest to the equator.

_____ 7. India is in the Southern Hemisphere.

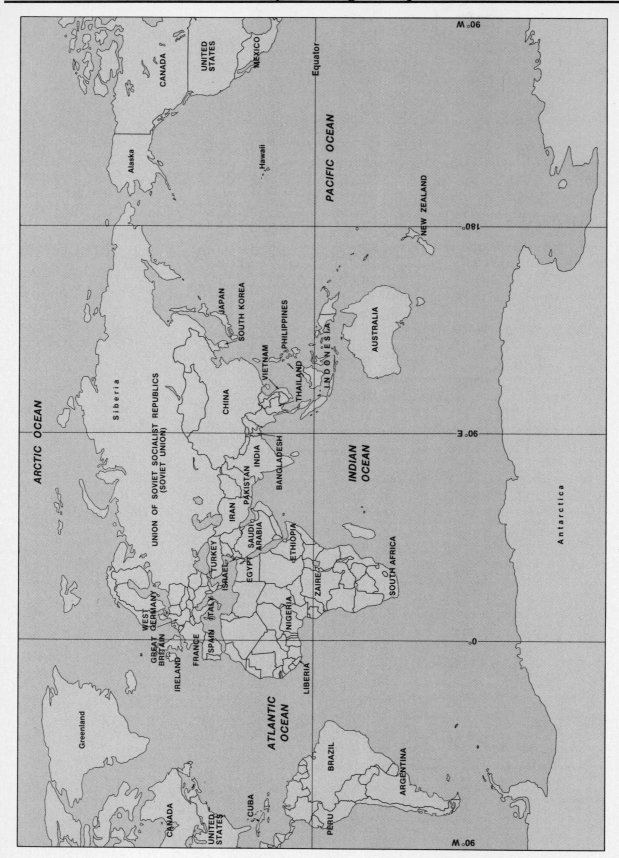

TOPIC 2
A World Context for American History: Working with Space

UNDERSTANDING THE MAP

Miller's cylindrical projection is used for this map. It creates the effect of a flat piece of paper rolled into a cylinder, which is then put around a globe so that it touches each place on the equator. A light source at the center of the earth then projects the outline of the contents on the paper. The image is accurate only at the equator. As it proceeds poleward it becomes more and more distorted.

WORKING WITH SPACE

1. Compare the size of Greenland with South America on this map. In reality, South America is _____ times as large. (a. two, b. three, c. five, d. eight)

2. The continent with the greatest area of distortion is _____.

3. One parallel and four meridians are indicated on this map. The equator, the parallel midway between the earth's _____ , crosses two continents: _____ and _____. Each of these continents has a large equatorial rain forest and basin drained by great rivers: the _____ and the _____.

4. Name the meridian most closely associated with the following geographic features:

   _____ **a.** Pacific Ocean   0°

   _____ **b.** Mississippi Delta   90° E

   _____ **c.** Ganges Delta   180°

   _____ **d.** London   90° W

5. Plan a cruise around the world starting from Chesapeake Bay and proceeding eastward to visit Rome, Athens, Bombay, Singapore, and Tokyo. Trace this route on the map. List the following geographic features in the order you will reach them: Panama Canal, Red Sea, Pacific Ocean, Caribbean Sea, Atlantic Ocean, Suez Canal, Mediterranean Sea, Indian Ocean, Strait of Malacca, Strait of Gibraltar, South China Sea.

6. The coming of Europeans to the Americas caused a great dislocation of peoples. The Native American Indians were decimated by Old World diseases and pushed out of many areas by the European invasion. The Europeans also imported slaves from Africa to the Americas. Place arrows on the map to indicate these three movements in North American history: the migration of Europeans, the retreat of Native Americans, and the forced migration of African slaves to the Western Hemisphere. Use an arrow with a dotted line to show the route of the first Americans from Siberia to Mexico. Then show later Pacific migration from China and Southeast Asia to the United States.

EXTENSIONS

One of the advantages of a cylindrical projection is that you can easily rearrange the map to give a different visual impression. You can call this version of the world map the Old World orientation. Use the three extra copies of this map found in Appendix I. Cut the first one along the prime meridian at 0° longitude. Then cut it at the margin and tape it together again at 90° West so that the new map has 180° at the center. Label it "World Map: Pacific Orientation." Cut the next map at 90° E and follow the same procedure so that 90° W is at the center. Label this map "World Map: American Orientation." Cut the third map along 180° and again follow the directions so that the prime meridian is in the center. Label this map "World Map: Atlantic Orientation."

Write a brief essay noting the advantages of the four versions of the world map (Old World, Pacific, American, and Atlantic orientations) for conceptualizing American history. Conclude by selecting the one you prefer and explain why you chose this particular version.

HarperCollins Publishers © 1991

ATLANTIC OCEAN

St. John
Connecticut
Hudson
Delaware
St. Lawrence
Susquehanna
Potomac
James
Lake Ontario
Lake Erie
Savannah
St. Johns
Lake Huron
Ohio
Cumberland
Tennessee
Alabama
Lake Michigan
Lake Superior
Wabash
Mississippi
Wisconsin
Illinois
Iowa
Mississippi
Gulf of Mexico
Arkansas
Red
Red
Brazos
Missouri
Platte
Pecos
Yellowstone
Rio Grande
Missouri
Green
Colorado
Gila
Snake
Humboldt
Great Salt Lake
Columbia
Sacramento
San Joaquin
PACIFIC OCEAN

400 Miles
200
400 Kilometers
200
0
0

PACIFIC OCEAN
100 Miles
100 Kilometers
0

Yukon
Gulf of Alaska
400 Miles
400 Kilometers
0
0
BERING SEA
PACIFIC OCEAN

HarperCollins Publishers © 1991

TOPIC 3
Geographic Context: River Basins

People who lived near rivers, William E. Wilson wrote in 1940, could not go for long without a visit to the riverbank. The novelist spoke for an earlier, rural America, but the magnetic attraction of rivers remains alive today. Wilson described one individual standing for hours watching the waters flow by on their journey to the sea. Why, he asked, was the river such an attraction? The river was beautiful, to be sure, but it also symbolized "eternal change within eternal changelessness." As such it reassured the watcher of "permanence and stability." Without rivers America would be a strange place, "shapeless, confusing, and without reason for being. . . ." (*The Wabash*, p. 6).

More prosaic reasons might be advanced for beginning a study of the geographical context of American history by focusing on its rivers, but Wilson's spiritual explanation in the end carries with it the most meaning.

The major rivers of the United States are labeled for you on this map. As you proceed through the study of American history you should come to know the location of each one. Topic 4 will help you test yourself on the names of individual rivers. This activity focuses more on the grouping of rivers into larger categories like basins and regions.

PLACES

1. The Continental Divide separates the waters flowing into the Atlantic and Pacific oceans. Draw a line on this map from Mexico to Canada showing the approximate location of the Continental Divide, and label it.

2. The Mississippi River and its tributaries form the major drainage basin in the United States. Begin at the Mississippi River delta and draw a line around the Mississippi River system. Label it and use a colored pencil to shade it. Note how it dominates the American interior.

3. A secondary continental divide separates the waters flowing southward into the Mississippi River system and those flowing northward into the Gulf of St. Lawrence and Hudson Bay. Draw a line showing this Midcontinent Divide and label it. Note that the Red River of the north sends its waters to the Hudson Bay.

4. Three long river systems reach from the Pacific Ocean deep into the American interior. Draw lines around the basins of the Colorado, the Columbia–Snake, and the Yukon river systems. The last, located on the inset map of Alaska, is navigable almost all the way across the state.

5. The Atlantic and Gulf coastal plains have major rivers spaced at regular intervals along the shoreline. Draw a line around the Atlantic coastal plain and label it.

WORKING WITH SPACE

1. The rivers of the Atlantic Coast provided a variety of passageways into the continent. They furnished access routes for a variety of separate colonies. Eventually, how many states would front on the Atlantic Ocean? _____

2. The Pacific Coast presents the opposite case. Only a few major rivers are present. Only three of the lower 48 states are on the Pacific Ocean: _____,

   _____,

   and_____.

3. The Great Basin centered in Utah and Nevada has no outlet to the sea. Its two major hydrographic features are the _____ River and the_____ Lake.

HarperCollins Publishers © 1991

ATLANTIC OCEAN

Gulf of Mexico

PACIFIC OCEAN

PACIFIC OCEAN

Gulf of Alaska

BERING SEA

PACIFIC OCEAN

TOPIC 4
Geographic Context: Rivers

BACKGROUND

In some ways this image presents the land as it was when people first arrived. Rivers were the primary organizing features on the landscape. They were yet to be named. Following their courses would lead to other regions and new places. Native Americans, European explorers, and pioneers all envisioned the continent in terms of its rivers.

The map and the discussion in Topic 3 form a unit with this activity and should be consulted from time to time as reference help is needed.

PLACES

Label the italicized rivers on the map:

1. *The St. Lawrence River* serves as the outlet for the Great Lakes. It afforded the first riverine avenue into the continent when Jacques Cartier explored it in 1535. Later it served as the major route for French penetration into North America.

2. *The Hudson River* is almost perpendicular to the St. Lawrence, flowing due south. It was navigable for early ocean-going vessels all the way upstream to the site of Albany. It served as the major axis of Dutch settlement and later as the foundation for New York City's commercial dominance.

3. *The Potomac River* led from Chesapeake Bay into the depths of the Appalachian mountains. Its location in the middle of the new nation and its orientation to the west made it a natural site for selection as the nation's capital.

4. *The St. Johns River* was the site for an early French colony in Florida in 1564. A year later the struggling settlement was wiped out by the Spanish and replaced with St. Augustine.

5. *The Mississippi River* was set upon in several different ways. Spanish explorers and adventurers approached its great valley from the south, from the Gulf Coastal Plain, and the Southwest in the half century following the landfall of Columbus.

6. The vast extent of the Mississippi River became known only in the late 17th century when French explorers reached its major tributaries after portaging from the Great Lakes basin. The *Wisconsin* and *Illinois* rivers were key tributaries for this approach.

8. The *Ohio River* and its tributaries provided a link between the Mississippi Valley and the European colonies along the Atlantic.

9. The western tributaries of the Mississippi River reach into dry regions. They characteristically have long narrow valleys, like the *Arkansas* and the *Red* rivers. The *Missouri River*, however, reaches behind the mountains to tap their well-watered western slopes.

10. The *Rio Grande* offered the Spanish in Mexico convenient access to North America. It was a major avenue of Hispanic cultural diffusion.

11. The *Colorado River* traces a long and rugged course but is the least populated major river valley in the lower 48 states.

12. The *Columbia–Snake* river system in the Northwest furnished Lewis and Clark with a route to the Pacific Ocean after they had pushed up the Missouri River to its western extremity.

13. The *Red River* of the north is part of the Arctic Ocean drainage (by way of Hudson Bay). It was the site of bonanza farming after 1875.

14. The greatest agricultural bonanza, however, is the Valley of California, drained by the *Sacramento* and *San Joaquin* rivers.

15. The *Yukon River* in Alaska is the third longest river in the United States, exceeded only by the Mississippi and the Missouri.

EXTENSIONS

Select one of these major rivers and develop an outline for a narrative account of the history of people in its valley. Start with the earliest Native American presence and come up to the present, dividing the topic into at least five major periods.

HarperCollins Publishers © 1991

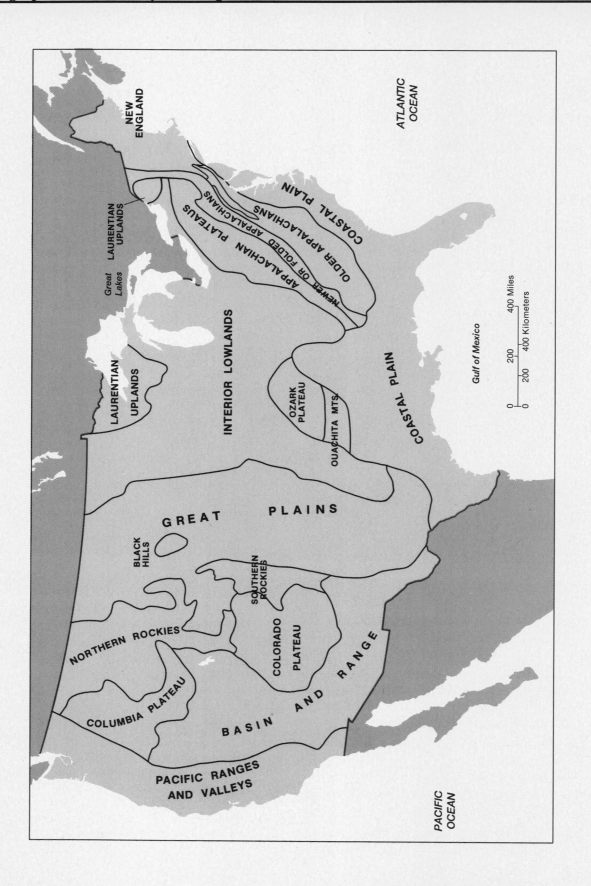

ATLANTIC OCEAN

NEW ENGLAND

LAURENTIAN UPLANDS

Great Lakes

LAURENTIAN UPLANDS

COASTAL PLAIN

OLDER APPALACHIANS

NEWER OR FOLDED APPALACHIANS

APPALACHIAN PLATEAUS

INTERIOR LOWLANDS

OZARK PLATEAU

OUACHITA MTS.

GREAT   PLAINS

COASTAL PLAIN

Gulf of Mexico

BLACK HILLS

SOUTHERN ROCKIES

NORTHERN ROCKIES

COLORADO PLATEAU

COLUMBIA PLATEAU

BASIN   AND   RANGE

PACIFIC RANGES AND VALLEYS

PACIFIC OCEAN

400 Miles

400 Kilometers

200

200

0

0

TOPIC 5
Geographic Context: Physical Regions

BACKGROUND

Regions are areas that have certain characteristics in common and are differentiated from surrounding places. Human activities lead to regional groupings on the land: the Corn Belt, an urban ghetto, or a manufacturing district. Physical regions are similar groupings based on natural processes, rooted mainly in geology but also affected by climate, soils, and vegetation.

It is often difficult to draw a precise boundary around a region and there are almost always exceptional places within the perimeter, but such generalization is necessary when dealing with space on a broad scale. A satisfactory division of the lower 48 states into physical regions would need at least 40 distinct areas. This map simplifies the scheme to present a even more generalized picture.

PLACES

Locate and label the following physical regions on your map.

1. Begin with the coastal regions of the nation. Along the Pacific there is a complex mixture of mountain ranges and long, narrow valleys. Label this area with the conglomerate title *"Pacific Ranges and Valleys."* The *Atlantic Coastal Plain* and *Gulf Coastal Plain* are low-lying areas except for *New England*, which is mostly a glaciated upland area.

2. West of the Atlantic Coastal Plain is the Appalachian system, divided into three major categories: *Older Appalachian Mountains*, Newer or *Folded Mountains*, and the *Appalachian Plateau* (in east-to-west order).

3. The middle of the continent is dominated by two extensive and fairly level regions: the *Interior Lowlands* south and west of the Great Lakes and the *Great Plains* extending from Mexico to Canada.

4. Several upland regions are scattered across the relatively level interior. The *Laurentian Uplands* are areas where the glaciers have exposed a hard core of very ancient rocks at either end of the Great Lakes. These rock formations had several favored locations around Lake Superior with very rich seams of iron ore.

5. The *Ozark Plateau* and the *Ouachita Mountains* below it are outlying segments of the Appalachian System.

6. The *Black Hills* are a detached segment of the Rocky Mountains.

7. The Rocky Mountains are divided into two major parts: the *Southern Rockies* and the *Northern Rockies*. Between them is South Pass, the passageway from the Great Plains to the intermontane plateaus.

8. An extensive plateau region lies between the Rocky Mountains and the Pacific Ranges (the Cascades and the Sierra Nevada). It is divided into three major regions: The *Columbia Plateau* in the north, the *Colorado Plateau* behind the Southern Rockies, and a large *Basin and Range* province where mountain ranges alternate with dry basins in a nearly regular pattern.

EXTENSIONS

The physiographic boundaries of North America seem to have a north-south orientation. Horace Greeley's admonition, "Go west, young man, go west," thus enabled a young adventurer to cross a dozen physiographic regions on a trip from New York to San Francisco.

Develop a proposal for a travelogue video in which a group of college students go by car from Boston to San Francisco, stopping from time to time to note the change of scenery. Label each scene by the physical region to be observed and select a location for photographing the region. Assemble notes, pictorial materials, and maps as you wish to make a complete portfolio to accompany your proposal.

HarperCollins Publishers © 1991

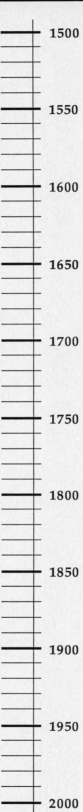

1500

1550

1600

1650

1700

1750

1800

1850

1900

1950

2000

HarperCollins Publishers © 1991

TOPIC 6
A Chronological Context for American History

BACKGROUND

There are three steps in developing a chronological context for any historical project, whether it be a survey course in American history, a study of a local community's past, or an autobiography. First, the historian must select certain events as key dates to understand the development of the topic at hand. Next, he or she must list these key events in chronological order. Such a list is called a chronology. The third step is to record these events on a measured timeline such as the one on the opposite page, to help develop a periodization scheme for the project.

Periods are created by historians to group events that are similar in character or that seem to be functionally part of the same development. Periods are to time like regions are to space. Both are invented by people to help them understand the things they experience. They don't exist in reality; they are mental constructs rather than lines on the ground or special days when trumpets sound at sunrise.

Because periods are mental constructs, each historian is free to develop a periodization scheme that suits his or her perception of reality. Different accounts might use different key events and turning points to construct new periods with fresh names. A familiar story like American history often acquires a standard set of key events, periods, and names that are helpful to have in mind as you proceed with your more detailed study, chapter by chapter and period by period.

WORKING WITH TIME

1. This timeline is set in the middle of the page to help you work with time. Key events are to be recorded at their precise location in the left-hand column. The space on the right-hand side is for the division of the story into various periods. Enter the Declaration of Independence on the left-hand side and then draw a line across the right-hand column at 1776. Label "The Colonial Period" before the Declaration vertically on the far right-hand edge of the page. Use "The National Period" for the time after 1776.

2. The founding of Jamestown in 1607 led to the first permanent English colony in America and the beginning of the European settlements that eventually would make up the United States. Record this key date on the timeline and draw another line across the right-hand column to separate the Aboriginal and the Colonial periods.

3. The Civil War (1861–1865) was the greatest crisis in American national history. Some historians emphasize how the war changed the nature of the Union by labeling the antebellum period "The Federal Union" and the post–1865 era as "The American Nation." Record this on your timeline.

4. The European discovery of America began in 1492 with the first voyage of Columbus. In 1498 John Cabot sailed along the eastern coast of North America. Coronado explored the region from New Mexico to Kansas in 1540–1542. St. Augustine was founded in 1565, and Santa Fe in 1607. Select one or two of these dates to record on your timeline.

5. Some key events in colonial history are the Mayflower Compact, 1620; the English conquest of New Netherland, 1664; the founding of Charleston, 1670; William Penn's Frame of Government, 1682; the Salem Witch Trials, 1692; the founding of Georgia, 1732; and the French and Indian War, 1754–1763. Choose several of these events to record on your timeline.

6. Use your textbook to find three or four key events for the national period of American history.

EXTENSIONS

Reflect on the events you have selected to place on your timeline. What do these choices indicate about your own experiences and your conception of history? If you were someone else, how might these selections have changed? Develop a list of five to ten observations on how the way you worked with time reflected your own personality and situation in life.

HarperCollins Publishers © 1991

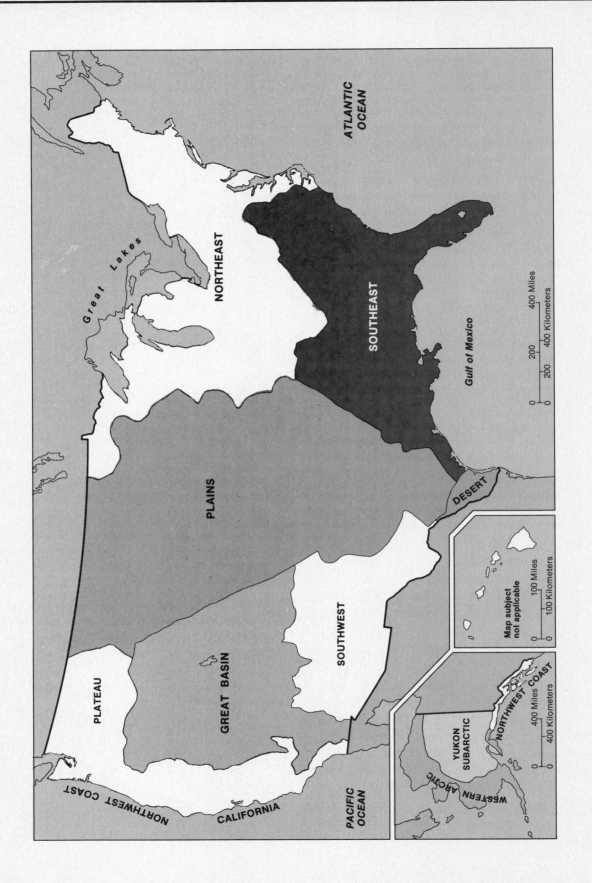

ATLANTIC OCEAN

NORTHEAST

Great Lakes

SOUTHEAST

Gulf of Mexico

400 Miles

400 Kilometers

200

200

0

0

PLAINS

DESERT

Map subject not applicable

100 Miles

100 Kilometers

0

0

SOUTHWEST

GREAT BASIN

PLATEAU

NORTHWEST COAST

400 Miles

400 Kilometers

0

0

YUKON SUBARCTIC

WESTERN ARCTIC

PACIFIC OCEAN

CALIFORNIA

NORTHWEST COAST

HarperCollins Publishers © 1991

TOPIC 7
Native American Culture Areas, A.D. 500–1300

BACKGROUND

Who was here on the eve of the European conquest? Can we divide the multitude of tribes into general groups? Where did they live? This map tries to answer some of these questions. Think of it as a generalized and simplified portrait of the peoples of America. It is adapted from two widely used schemes that can be conveniently located in Harold E. Driver, *Indians of North America* (2nd ed. 1969) and Alvin M. Josephy, Jr., *The Indian Heritage of America* (1968).

The 12 culture areas simply indicate that most of the people living in the area followed a similar way of life. Culture areas do not necessarily indicate common ancestry or similar language families.

PLACES

Label the following on the map:

1. Kodiak Island, Alaska, the large island at the entrance to Cook Inlet; by 100 B.C. its Pacific Eskimo culture was based on the hunting of sea animals, including whales.

2. Chaco Canyon, in northwestern New Mexico, the hub of Anasazi culture, reached its peak about 1100 A.D. and had an extensive irrigated agricultural system and a well-developed network of roads.

3. Cahokia, Illinois, on the Mississippi River opposite the site of St. Louis, was the largest Native American settlement in the area that later became the United States. By 1150 A.D. it had a population of about 10,000 people.

4. Moundville, Alabama, in the west central part of the state, succeeded Cahokia as the largest settlement north of Mexico. When Columbus discovered America it probably had a population of between 2000 and 3000 people.

5. Hopewell, in south central Ohio, gave its name to an advanced Woodland culture that reached its peak about 200 A.D.

6. The Iroquois Confederation, south of Lake Ontario, across New York State, was a grouping of related tribes apparently based on trading patterns. A formal political confederation did not occur until later, about the time of European contact.

7. California, with its great variety of environments, produced about 500 distinct cultures by 1500 A.D., almost all of them based on hunting and gathering. The population density of this culture area exceeded that of all of the others. Label it "Land of 500 Cultures."

WORKING WITH SPACE

Match the culture area with the historic tribe:

_____	1. Winnebago	A. California
_____	2. Hopi	B. Southwest
_____	3. Cherokee	C. Western Arctic
_____	4. Spokane	D. Great Basin
_____	5. Pomonan	E. Plateau
_____	6. Paiute	F. Northeast
_____	7. Aleut	G. Southeast

EXTENSIONS

Use a blank timeline from the appendix to lay out the temporal sequence of Native American cultural patterns. Locate the dates on the chart when these settlements reached their peak: Chaco Canyon, Cahokia, Moundville, Hopewell, and Iroquois Confederacy. Add two or more significant events for the Native American experience in the area that is now your home state.

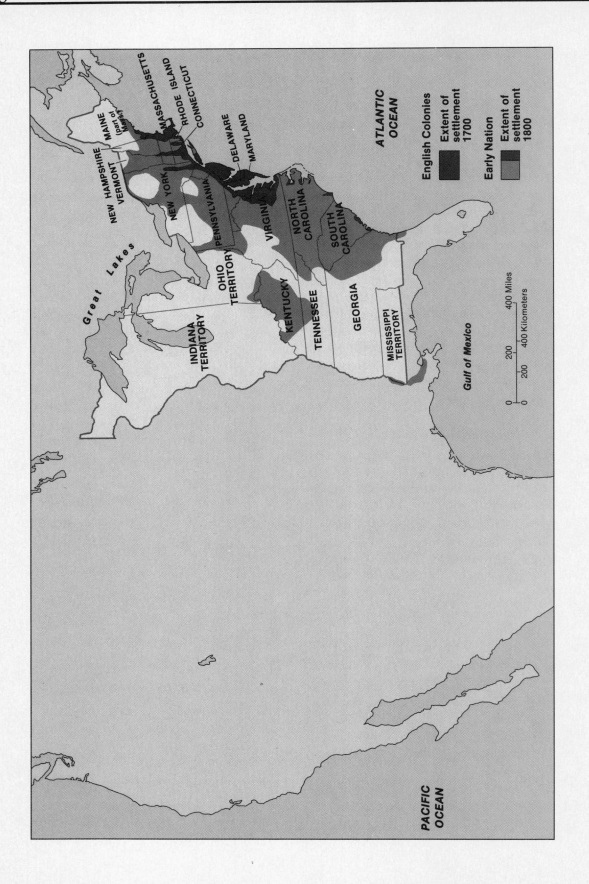

English Colonies

Extent of settlement 1700

Early Nation

Extent of settlement 1800

ATLANTIC OCEAN

MAINE (part of Mass.)

NEW HAMPSHIRE
VERMONT
MASSACHUSETTS
RHODE ISLAND
CONNECTICUT
DELAWARE
MARYLAND
NEW YORK
PENNSYLVANIA
VIRGINIA
NORTH CAROLINA
SOUTH CAROLINA

Great Lakes

OHIO TERRITORY
INDIANA TERRITORY
KENTUCKY
TENNESSEE
GEORGIA
MISSISSIPPI TERRITORY

Gulf of Mexico

400 Miles
200
400 Kilometers
200
0
0

PACIFIC OCEAN

TOPIC 8

English Colonial and American National Settlement, 1700 and 1800

BACKGROUND

Settlement maps such as these carry a fundamental impediment to historical understanding. The images convey the impression that people came from the Old World and set up new communities in a virgin land, represented as a vast void on the map. Actually the process was much more complicated, because in almost every case native peoples were being dispossessed in the process. Terms like *invasion* or *conquest*, now commonly used in the historical literature, apply to the very same process designated as "settlement" on these maps.

Historical maps often depict change over time. This one shows the extent of English colonial settlement in 1700 and American national settlement in 1800. The nucleus along the coast expanded into the broader area in a century of expansion.

PLACES:
English Colonial Settlement, 1700

1. The early English colonies clustered along the Atlantic seaboard at a respectful distance from Spanish claims to the south and French settlements to the north. Label the French and the Spanish colonies in 1700 on your map. Which nation seemed destined to control the Great Lakes? _____ Which one seemed likely to dominate the Mississippi River? _____

2. In 1700, two tongues of settlement extended into the interior in a northern direction. Both followed major rivers, the Hudson and the Connecticut. Which was first settled by the Dutch? _____

3. Delaware Bay, first settled by Swedish colonists, became the gateway to the Quaker settlements. The major Quaker city was _____ . Label it on your map.

4. Label Chesapeake Bay on your map. Which two colonies were located on this long inlet of the sea? _____ and _____ .

5. South of the Chesapeake, the English settlements were not contiguous, but were spread out like a chain of islands. Label Charleston. Note that it was not only the English settlement farthest south in 1700, but also the one farthest _____ .

PLACES:
Early National Period, 1800

6. Georgia was first settled in _____ . Label Savannah on the map.

7. In the century after 1700 the English peoples in America recorded several significant achievements beyond the triumph in the Great War for Empire and the winning of independence. First, they filled the Atlantic _____ _____ and the eastern portion of the _____ region with farms and towns. Label Charlotte, North Carolina, which was settled in the 1740s, incorporated in 1768, and is said to have declared its independence from Britain as early as May 20, 1775. Is Charlotte farther west than Pittsburgh? _____ .

8. Secondly, in the aftermath of independence, American settlements crossed the mountains and spilled into the Ohio Valley, creating an island of frontier communities in _____ and _____ . Label Lexington, Kentucky. Which two early cities on the Ohio River were close to Lexington? _____ , Ohio and _____ , Kentucky.

9. The direction of settlement was set in a _____ ward flow. Little subsequent expansion occurred to the _____ or to the _____ . Locate and label Pittsburgh, then called the "gateway to the West," at the source of the _____ River.

10. By 1800, the Old Northwest was divided into two territories: _____ and _____ . Label the Old Northwest.

HarperCollins Publishers © 1991

17

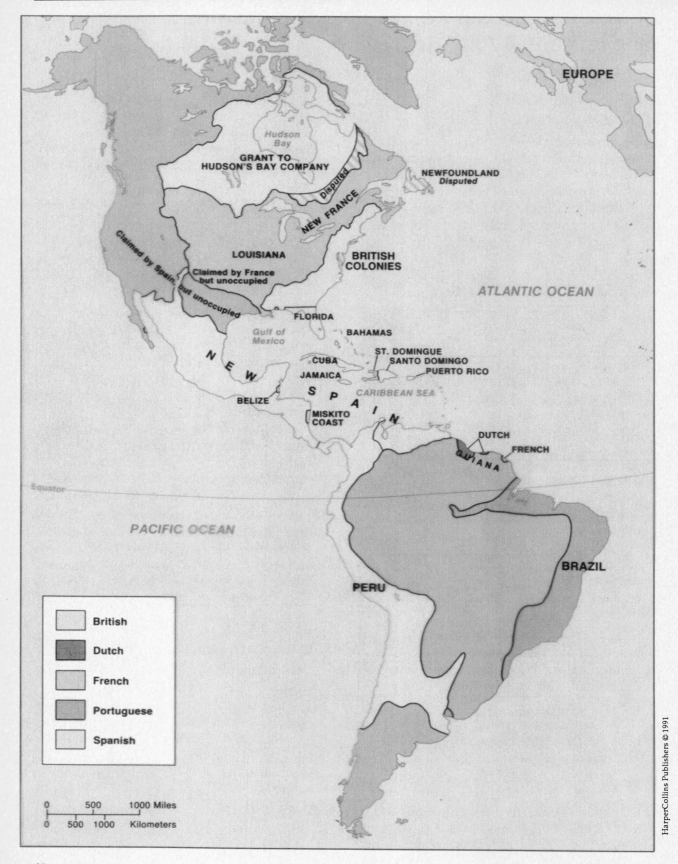

EUROPE

Hudson Bay

GRANT TO HUDSON'S BAY COMPANY

Disputed

NEWFOUNDLAND
Disputed

NEW FRANCE

LOUISIANA

Claimed by Spain, but unoccupied

Claimed by France but unoccupied

BRITISH COLONIES

ATLANTIC OCEAN

FLORIDA

Gulf of Mexico

BAHAMAS

N E W

CUBA

JAMAICA

ST. DOMINGUE
SANTO DOMINGO
PUERTO RICO

S P A I N

CARIBBEAN SEA

BELIZE

MISKITO COAST

DUTCH
FRENCH

G U I A N A

Equator

PACIFIC OCEAN

BRAZIL

PERU

British

Dutch

French

Portuguese

Spanish

| 0 | 500 | 1000 Miles |
| 0 | 500 | 1000 | Kilometers |

HarperCollins Publishers © 1991

TOPIC 9
A Hemispheric View: American Colonies in 1700

BACKGROUND

This map uses the whole hemisphere for its base because the story of colonial America demands a broader canvas than North America standing alone. To focus only on North America would miss a cartographic opportunity, and it would permit a parochial outlook to obscure the idea of America in the Age of Empire.

PLACES AND DATES

1. British interest in the Americas about 1700 was divided into three sectors. First, there were the mainland colonies along the Atlantic seaboard, extending from New Hampshire to Carolina. Second, there was a broad extent of land in the North devoted to the fur-trading interests of the Hudson's Bay Company. Finally there were a series of small, but highly valued, colonies grouped around the Caribbean Sea. Record on your map: Jamestown, 1607; Belize, 1638; the establishment of Jamaica as a British colony, 1665; and the Hudson's Bay Company grant, 1670.

2. The Dutch had been expelled from New Netherland (1664) and were then confined to several small outposts on the northern flank of South America. Label Surinam and record its date, 1667.

3. The French had some interests in the Caribbean region and in South America, but the major portion of their American empire reached from the Gulf of St. Lawrence to the Mississippi Valley. Label Sault Ste. Marie and the date of its founding, 1641.

4. The Portuguese had, by 1700, occupied lands west of old Line of Demarcation (1494) that crossed the mouth of the Amazon River. Label Sao Paulo (1532) and Pernambuco (1536).

5. Spanish America was divided into the viceroyalities of New Spain and Peru. The former included most of the Caribbean islands. Label Mexico City (1521), Lima (1535), and Buenos Aires (1535).

6. Use a series of colors to identify the various imperial claims in 1700. Be sure to color the key as well.

WORKING WITH SPACE AND TIME

True or False

_____ 1. The French established an outpost at the straits between Lake Superior and Lake Huron before New Amsterdam became New York.

_____ 2. Mexico City became a Spanish center 180 years before the founding of Jamestown.

_____ 3. Spain dominated the Atlantic coast of South America in 1700.

_____ 4. Three nations had established colonies on the Pacific Coast of the Americas by 1700.

_____ 5. In 1700 the viceroyalities of New Spain and Peru had jurisdiction extending from the Atlantic to the Pacific Ocean.

_____ 6. Pernambuco in 1700 was the American colony located farthest to the east.

HarperCollins Publishers © 1991

A PLAN of the CITY and ENVIRONS of NEW YORK

as they were in the Years 1742...1743 and 1744 Drawn by D..G. in the 76th year of his age who had at this time a perfect & correct recollection of every part of the same.

REFERENCES.

1 Fort George
2 Governor's House
3 Barracks & Guard House
4 Secretary's Office
5 Governor's Garden
6 Half Moon Battery
7 City Hall
8 Watch House
9 Old Dutch Church
10 New
11 Trinity
12 French
13 Lutheran
14 Presbyterian Meeting
15 Baptist
16 Quaker Meeting
17 Synagogue
18 Broad Street Market
19 Centre
20 Old Ship
21 Boat
22 Flag
23 Oswego
24 Poor House
25 Palisades
26 Block House
27 Powder
28 Slaughter
29 Rutgers Sugar House
30 Bally's Ship Yard
31 Rivers Ship Yard
32 Lathams
33 A Rutgers Brew House
34 H Rutgers
35 H Benson's
36 H Rutgers
37 Van Brooks Tan Yard
38 Anthony's
39 Beari & Stearns
40 Roome & Ryes
41 Van Pelt's Rope Walks
42 Fen Pole
43 Corneluss Pottery
44 Remsney & Corlius Battery
45 A Rutgers Farm
46 Bayard's Farm
47 J Delancey's
48 H Rutgers
49 Murthoens
50 Iews Bur ying Ground
51 Public Wells
52 City Gates
53 Gov Leisler buried here
54 Bastinaus built here
55 Plot Negro's burnt here
56 Plot Negro Gibbeted
57 Plot Hughson Gibbeted
58 Spring Garden
59 Bowling Green
60 Adam Van Der Berg's Farm

Fort George

NORTH RIVER

EAST RIVER

Collect

HarperCollins Publishers © 1991

TOPIC 10
New York City, 1744

BACKGROUND

David Grim's "A Plan of the City and Environs of New York as they were in the Years 1742, 1743, and 1744" was not drawn until August, 1813. The "old settler" was then in his 76th year of age but he had, according to the lithograph, "a perfect and correct recollection of every part" of the town. Similar maps, "reconstructed from memory," exist for many American cities.

All maps reflect a time gap between the date of the original data and the time of publication. A year or two could be expected, but the nearly seven decades that separated this map from its subject permitted a good deal of subjectivity to enter the plan. Added to this was the tendency of the publisher to "pretty things up" to produce an appealing print. Thus the city pictured on the map is an orderly settlement colored in pleasant hues and composed of trim, neat buildings such as those illustrated at the top.

These reconstructions must be used with care, but they help us visualize the physical layout of a former settlement. Who had better credentials to draw a retrospective map of the city than one who lived there at the time?

WORKING WITH SPACE

1. The close association between the English colonial cities and access to the Atlantic Ocean is very evident on this map. Start your analysis of this map by coloring the hydrographic features blue. Label the Hudson River, the East River, and the Collect. Use an arrow to show the direction toward the mouth of New York harbor.

2. The island divides into two distinct parts, the city at the lower end and the rural "environs" north of the palisade. There is a broad transition zone between city and countryside. It seems that the wall has been placed so that the city can keep growing. Label Manhattan Island and the city of New York. Use an orange color to show the built up part of the city and the city wall.

3. Use various shades of green to color the open spaces within the city and the rural environs.

4. New York in 1744 was a small walking city. Everyone could easily walk about the town. Draw a scale of miles on the map. The distance from the tip of Manhattan (Half Moon Battery) to Wall Street is about 1/2 mile. From Fort George to the wall is about 1-1/4 miles.

5. Label Wall Street, which traces the wall of early New Amsterdam. It runs across the island about a third of the way between the battery and the palisade, from Trinity Church with its yard on the west to Centre Street Market on the East River.

QUIZ

New York City in 1744: (complete the statement by writing in the blank *Did* or *Did Not*).

1. _____ follow a gridiron plan.

2. _____ provide for defense from attack by land and sea.

3. _____ support several different churches.

4. _____ give evidence of being a commercial center.

5. _____ occupy most of Manhattan Island.

EXTENSIONS

Note that several of the structures mentioned above are pictured on the print: Fort George and Trinity Church. Try to find a larger copy of this print or similar images that show the structure of colonial cities. Use one of these maps or views to write a brief description of the specific site. Cast the essay in the form of a commentary on the print.

HarperCollins Publishers © 1991

Great Lakes

QUEBEC

Quebec
Dec. 31, 1775

Arnold

MAINE
(Mass.)

Montreal

Burgoyne

N.H.

Howe
evacuates

N.Y.

Bemis Heights
Oct. 7, 1777

Lexington
Apr. 19, 1775

Boston

MASS.

CONN.

R.I.

Ft. Detroit

PA.

Trenton
Dec. 26, 1776

Howe

Brandywine
Sept. 11, 1777

New York
occupied July 3, 1776

MD.

N.J.

DEL.

Clark

Lafayette

Vincennes
Feb. 25, 1779

Ohio R.

VA.

Virginia Capes
Sept. 5-9, 1781

Cahokia

Yorktown
Oct. 19, 1781

de Grasse
from the West Indies

THE WAR
AT SEA

Kaskaskia

Guilford
Courthouse
Mar. 15, 1781

N.C.

Cornwallis

SPANISH LOUISIANA

Mississippi R.

Kings Mtn.
Oct. 7, 1780

Clinton and
Cornwallis

Cowpens
Jan. 17, 1781

S.C.

Charleston
May 10, 1780

GA.

ATLANTIC OCEAN

W. FLA.

E. FLA.

Gulf of Mexico

○	Chronological sequence
←	American troop movements
✹	American victories
←	British troop movements
✸	British victories

0   300 Miles
0   300 Kilometers

HarperCollins Publishers © 1991

TOPIC 11
The War for Independence

BACKGROUND

In U.S. history the whole movement from 13 colonies to a unified, independent nation is called the American Revolution. The military aspect is the Revolutionary War or the War for American Independence. Armed conflict has a specific focus and can be assigned particular dates, locations, and significant events. The military events leading to American independence can also be seen in a broader perspective, as part of a long series of wars between France and England. From this viewpoint the center of the stage was often the sea, not the American continent.

PLACES AND DATES

1. Each major battle is labeled on this map and a blank circle next to the site is provided for you to number each of the events in chronological order. Howe's evacuation of Boston, for example, should be numbered 3. Complete the rest of the sequence.

2. Use a color code to distinguish the American and British victories.

WORKING WITH SPACE AND TIME

1. Name the battle best identified with the following famous phrases:

   a. "The shot heard 'round the world" (Ralph Waldo Emerson) _____

   b. "The World Turned Upside Down" (popular song) _____

2. Note that the major events of the war can be divided into three theaters: North, South, and West. In which theater did the following battles occur?

   a. King's Mountain _____

   b. Vincennes_____

   c. Charleston _____

   d. Bemis Heights _____

3. Benedict Arnold led the American invasion of Canada, which ended in a battle at

   _____.

4. The last major battle of the war in America was at _____ on _____. Here the British General _____ surrendered to combined patriot and French forces. The French hero _____ was present next to Washington.

5. According to this map, most of the Ohio River Valley was claimed by the state of

   _____.

1550

1575

1600

1625

1650

1675

1700

1725

1750

1775

1800

TOPIC 12
A Chronological Context for Early America

BACKGROUND

By definition a colony is controlled by a mother country and its history is bound to reflect changes that occur at the imperial seat. Therefore, to develop a chronological context for early American history, use one side of the timeline for key dates in the colonies and list similar events in Europe on the other side. Because our focus is on the 13 colonies along the mid–Atlantic coast, English history will be emphasized and we can set the inclusion years as 1550–1800.

WORKING WITH TIME

1. First draw lines across the entire page at the years 1600, 1700, and 1800. Then label in vertical fashion the 16th, 17th, and 18th centuries at the far right-hand margin.

2. Record the following key dates in American colonial history:

1587	Roanoke Colony
1607	Jamestown established
1619	Arrival of first African Americans
1620	Mayflower Compact
1630	Boston founded
1632	Maryland grant
1664	New Amsterdam became New York
1670	Charleston founded
1681	Pennsylvania grant
1686	Dominion of New England
1692	Witchcraft trials
1732	*Poor Richard's Almanack*
1734	Great Awakening begins in New England
1754–63	French and Indian War
1765	Stamp Act
1776	Declaration of Independence
1787	Constitutional Convention

3. Now use the right-hand side of the page to record the following reigns of English monarchs:

1558–1603	Elizabeth I
1603–1625	James I
1625–1649	Charles I
1649–1658	Puritan Revolution
1660–1685	Charles II
1685–1688	James II
1688–1689	Glorious Revolution
1689–1702	William III and Mary
1702–1714	Anne
1714–1727	George I
1727–1760	George II
1760–1840	George III

4. True or False

____ a. Jamestown was named after the reigning English monarch.

____ b. African Americans came to Virginia before the Mayflower came to New England.

____ c. The Dominion of New England was associated with James II.

____ d. The Salem witchcraft trials came at a time of political change.

____ e. The Great Awakening was connected with Oliver Cromwell.

____ f. During the French and Indian War a new king was crowned.

____ g. George III was deposed for the loss of the 13 colonies.

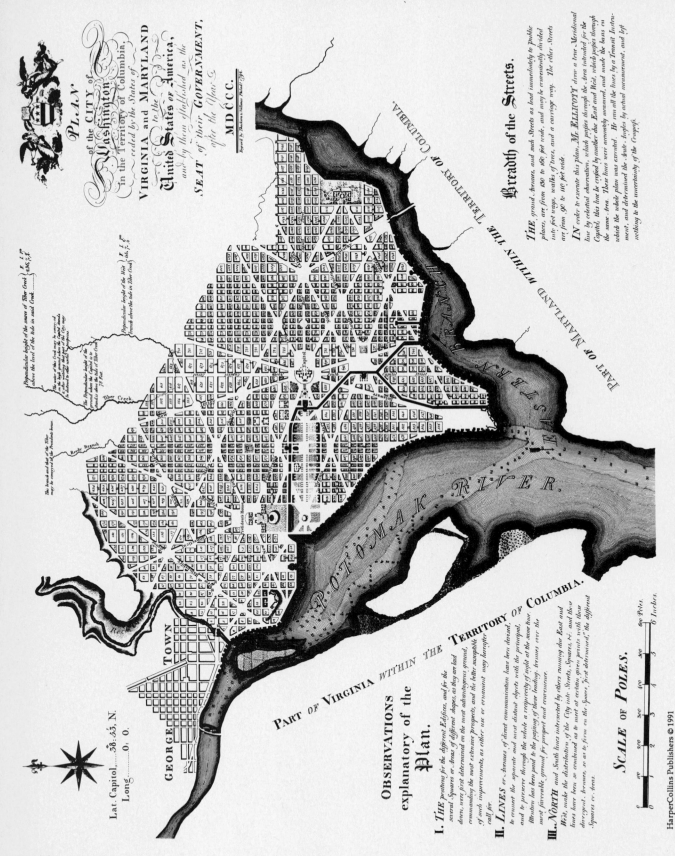

TOPIC 13
L'Enfant's Plan for the National Capitol

BACKGROUND

The founders of the nation hoped that Congress would be able to meet in a separate capital city away from the local pressures that were to be found in any city or state. A special federal district was therefore proposed under the Articles of Confederation. It became a reality when the new Congress under the Constitution empowered George Washington to select a location. He chose a site at the end of the tidewater on the Potomac River, then near the center of the nation. The place selected also had a distinct orientation to the west.

Washington chose architect-engineer Pierre L'Enfant to plan the city and appointed three commissioners to sell lots and erect the necessary public buildings. This 1792 version of the master plan shows the city as it was supposed to appear in 1800. Land sales, however, were much slower than expected; L'Enfant and the Commission argued; and some changes had to be made. Nevertheless, our national capital clearly follows this original plan.

WORKING WITH SPACE

1. The public buildings were to be located on the best sites with respect to views and prospects. Locate and label the Capitol and the Executive Mansion (later called the White House).

2. Georgetown was a community that already existed on the site. Note how it was connected to the plan but not made its central focus. Georgetown was at the head of navigation on the Potomac River where a bridge was located, symbolically connecting the North and the South. Label the Georgetown Bridge.

3. Note that the mall, which faced westward, was to be lined with public buildings. Label the "Mall" and use an arrow to point toward the west at the left-hand margin of the page.

4. As for many seaports located on a coastal plain, drainage was an important consideration in the planning of the capitol city. Locate and label the system of canals originally used for surface drainage.

5. A diagonal street was named for each of the original states plus Kentucky and Vermont. Label Pennsylvania Avenue, which connects the Executive Mansion with the Capitol, and Massachusetts Avenue, the longest street on the map.

CAPITOL COMMENTARY

1. The Washington Monument was erected due south of the Executive Mansion and west of the capitol. The space between these landmarks became known as the Federal Triangle. _____ Avenue forms the hypotenuse of this figure.

2. What part of the federal district suggests by its name that it originated before the American Revolution? _____ , which was named for the English _____ .

3. The small numbers in the Potomac River are soundings indicating the depth of the water. They end at Georgetown because it marks the _____ .

4. The "Territory of Columbia" included land that was part of two states: _____ and _____ .

5. Massachusetts Avenue extends from Rock Creek to a site for public buildings on the _____ , now called the Anacostia River.

EXTENSIONS

The modern consensus is that Pierre L'Enfant's plan for a capitol city proved to be very useful. Develop an essay suggesting the reasons for this success. Include a copy of the plan as part of your essay. You may want to include a modern map of Washington, D.C. as well.

Territorial Growth, 1800–1850

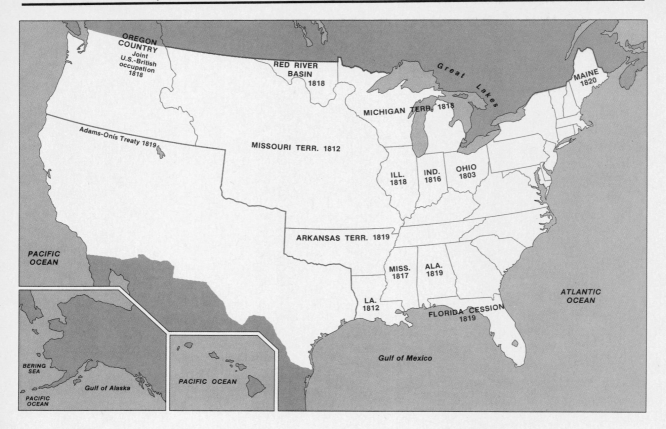

OREGON COUNTRY Joint U.S.-British occupation 1818

RED RIVER BASIN 1818

Great Lakes

MAINE 1820

MICHIGAN TERR. 1818

Adams-Onis Treaty 1819

MISSOURI TERR. 1812

ILL. 1818

IND. 1816

OHIO 1803

PACIFIC OCEAN

ARKANSAS TERR. 1819

MISS. 1817

ALA. 1819

ATLANTIC OCEAN

LA. 1812

FLORIDA CESSION 1819

BERING SEA

Gulf of Alaska

PACIFIC OCEAN

PACIFIC OCEAN

Gulf of Mexico

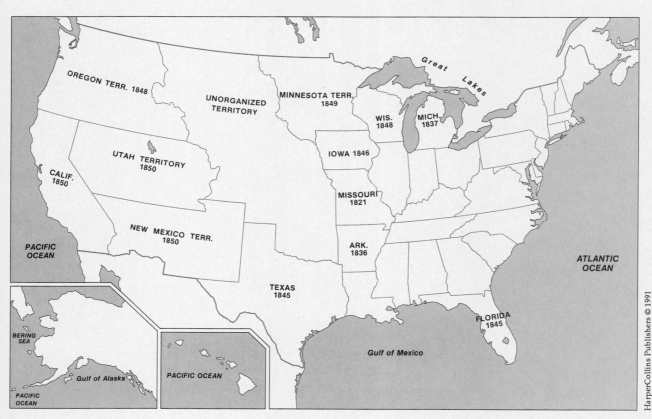

OREGON TERR. 1848

UNORGANIZED TERRITORY

MINNESOTA TERR. 1849

Great Lakes

WIS. 1848

MICH. 1837

UTAH TERRITORY 1850

IOWA 1846

CALIF. 1850

MISSOURI 1821

NEW MEXICO TERR. 1850

ARK. 1836

PACIFIC OCEAN

ATLANTIC OCEAN

TEXAS 1845

BERING SEA

Gulf of Alaska

PACIFIC OCEAN

PACIFIC OCEAN

FLORIDA 1845

Gulf of Mexico

HarperCollins Publishers © 1991

TOPIC 14
Territorial Growth, 1800–1850

BACKGROUND

The territorial expansion of the United States across the continent is one of the major themes of its history. The processes of acquisition and annexation went hand in hand with those of settlement and development. The vague overarching theme of Manifest Destiny gave the whole enterprise a higher calling and a lofty purpose beyond the quest for personal gain and national aggrandizement. The idea of one polity ruling North America from coast to coast dates back to the English visions of the 17th century.

Two centuries later, textbooks of American history featured maps showing the territorial growth of the nation. In the 1850s, however, expansion often provoked great issues for debate. The Civil War settled the matter and transformed these maps of national expansion into celebrations of the American way. A consensus soon emerged that the process of continental expansion was inevitable, the will of the Almighty. The debate then turned to overseas expansion.

WORKING WITH SPACE

1. The first map shows a remarkable expansion of territory for the new nation. In two decades the United States added four major areas to its territories and it achieved these results largely through diplomatic channels. Use color to designate the Louisiana Purchase, the Florida Cession, the Red River Basin, and the Oregon Country. The _____ was the largest in terms of territory and also was a necessary prelude to obtaining the others.

2. Between 1800 and 1820 seven new states were added to the Union. Three of these were in the Old Northwest: _____ , _____ , and _____ .

3. The three new states north of the Ohio River were balanced by three in the South: _____ , _____ , and _____ .

4. Maine, admitted in 1820, seemed to upset the balance between the North and the South. However, the map catches the situation in the midst of the maneuvering for the compromise that resulted in the subsequent admission of _____ in 1821.

5. In 1820 only one state, _____ , was located west of the Mississippi River and only two territories, _____ and _____ , were located east of the Father of Waters.

6. The second map shows the extent of the nation in 1850 after the Mexican Cession and the 1846 treaty with Great Britain. The _____ parallel was used as the northern boundary from Lake of the Woods to the Pacific Ocean, except for _____ Island.

7. In 1850 the southern boundary of Texas had been established at the _____ . West of the 109th meridian the final boundary with Mexico had not yet been finalized. The _____ Purchase would round out the extent of the lower 48 states in _____ .

8. With the admission of _____ , _____ , and _____ , all of the lands east of the Mississippi River had achieved statehood by 1850.

9. In 1845 the largest of the lower 48 states joined the Union. _____ extended about a _____ of the distance between the oceans and almost _____ of the distance between Mexico and British North America.

10. _____ was the first state to be located on the Pacific Ocean.

HarperCollins Publishers © 1991

ATLANTIC
OCEAN

Extent of
settlement
1850

Great Lakes

OHIO

INDIANA

MICHIGAN

ILLINOIS

WISCONSIN

IOWA

MISSOURI

ARKANSAS

MISSISSIPPI

ALABAMA

FLORIDA

LOUISIANA

Gulf of Mexico

400 Miles

200

0

400 Kilometers

200

0

MINNESOTA
TERRITORY

UNORGANIZED

TEXAS

OREGON
TERRITORY

UTAH TERRITORY

NEW MEXICO TERRITORY

CALIFORNIA

PACIFIC
OCEAN

HarperCollins Publishers © 1991

TOPIC 15
Extent of Settlement, 1850: U.S. Nationals

BACKGROUND

This map is a classic document in the mold of the frontier thesis. A quotation like the following might initiate a useful discussion:

"In a sense, American history up to our own day has been colonial history, the colonization of the Great West. This ever retreating frontier of free land is the key to American development." (Frederick Jackson Turner, "Problems in American History," *Aegis*, VII, November 4, 1892, p. 48).

WORKING WITH SPACE

1. The orderly process by which lands were sold and new communities founded is strikingly apparent on this map. Note how compact the settled portion of the nation actually was in 1850. Label the center of population according to the census of 1850. It is midway between Marietta, Ohio, and Charleston, Virginia (now West Virginia). Although still east of the _____ River, it was steadily marching westward, moving 80 miles to the west by the next census.

2. The major outlying islands of U.S. national settlement are all easily explained. One marks the Falls of St. Anthony on the _____ River, another is the Mormon settlement near the _____ , and a third traces the old line of Spanish settlement along the_____ Coast, with an extension inland to the gold region.

3. Note that although there were outposts of European settlements in the Rio Grande Valley, most of the people living there were Native Americans and not considered citizens.

4. The settlements in the Indian Territory in the Oklahoma region also do not show up in the census data on which this map is based. This explains the straight line at the western edge of _____ and

_____ .

5. The nation in 1850 had a northern and a southern, as well as a western, frontier. The site of Miami, Florida, was over _____ hundred miles from the frontier line.

PLACES

Locate the following key cities of the United States in 1850:

1. Pacific Coast: San Francisco
2. Gulf Coast: New Orleans
3. Atlantic Coast: Boston, Brooklyn, New York, Philadelphia, Baltimore
4. Ohio and Mississippi rivers: Pittsburgh, Cincinnati, Louisville, St. Louis
5. Great Lakes: Buffalo, Chicago, Cleveland, Detroit, Milwaukee
6. Inland: Albany, Richmond

EXTENSIONS

Select one of the cities on your map and describe its relationship with frontier regions in the period 1820–1850. What geographical factors influenced the dynamic between this city and the frontier?

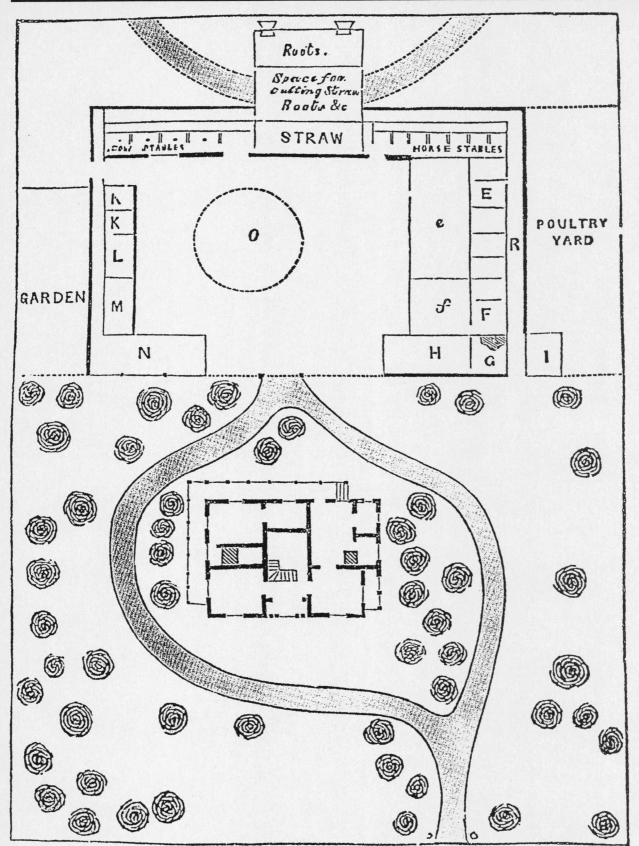

TOPIC 16
Farmery, House, and Gardens, 1852

BACKGROUND

The Farmer's and Emigrant's Hand-Book, from which this plan for a typical farmstead was taken, appeared in 1852. The volume was a typical compendium of advice for a person thinking about becoming a pioneer and planning to build a farmstead on the frontier. Similar volumes were soon issued by the railroads to help settle the lands they received as subsidies from the federal government. Toward the end of the century various state agencies joined in the production of "how-to" books on settlement and farming.

Some of the advice, of course, was worth more than others. This particular volume was so general in nature and attempted to be so wide in its application that the modern reader is apt to be very critical of its concept. Perhaps it was used at the time as the basis for discussion rather than as a recipe to be followed exactly to the letter. In any event the farmstead pictured here was seldom actually built according to plan, even in the Midwest where most of the advice seems to apply most directly.

The general thrust of the suggestions was to think of the farm as a work station that should be laid out in the most convenient manner, using machinery and expert knowledge. The word *farmery* was mainly a British term but it also sounded like *factory*. Although the relative size and arrangement of the structures would vary, "according to circumstances," their proper placement, it was claimed, could cut in half the labor of feeding animals and processing produce.

WORKING WITH SPACE

1. The farmstead is neatly divided into two parts, the house, including grounds, and the farmery. Label the Farmery and the Farm House.

2. A looped driveway extends around both sides of the house to reach the farmyard. The natural curve of the road contrasts with the angular rigidity of the house, the farmery, and even the lot. Select a spot for a choice ornamental shrub and mark it with an "X" on the map.

3. The house itself presents a symmetrical facade to the road that probably ran along the front lot line perpendicular to the entry drive. Note the entry hall in the center of the house, which contained a formal staircase to the bedrooms above. To the right and left of the entry are a pair of rooms for formal entertaining. Label these rooms "The Formal Area."

4. The farmery consists of a farmyard with a manure pit (O) surrounded by a series of buildings, each having a special function. Beyond the buildings were a garden on one side and a poultry yard on the other. In the center was the barn. Label these items.

5. Stables for the cows are to the left of the barn, stables for the horses to the right. The left-hand row of buildings was made up of a calf-house (K), a workshop (L), an equipment shed (M), and a wagon shed (N). Label these structures.

6. The right-hand row of buildings accommodated sheep (E) and pigs (F), each with their own fenced area in the farm yard. At the front of this structure were sheds for storing wood (H) and boiling roots (G). A long, narrow corn crib (R) came between the poultry house (I) and the right wing of the farmery. Label these structures.

7. To modern sensibilities the location of the manure pile would be questionable, but its central location was a key to efficient farming. It was to be about two feet below the surrounding buildings. Cleanings from the stables were to be removed each day "in a large boxed wheelbarrow, and straw and marsh muck supplied as needed" (p. 72).

Indicate with an arrow on the map the most desirable wind direction for the comfort of the household on a hot summer night.

EXTENSIONS

Compose a daily entry in a diary or write a letter to someone in an eastern city describing life on a farm such as this.

HarperCollins Publishers © 1991

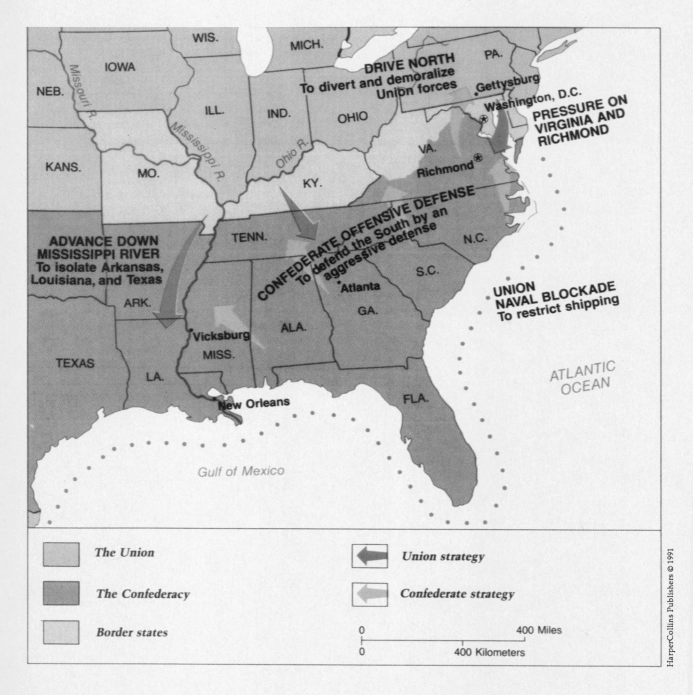

DRIVE NORTH
To divert and demoralize
Union forces

PRESSURE ON
VIRGINIA AND
RICHMOND

CONFEDERATE OFFENSIVE DEFENSE
To defend the South by an
aggressive defense

ADVANCE DOWN
MISSISSIPPI RIVER
To isolate Arkansas,
Louisiana, and Texas

UNION
NAVAL BLOCKADE
To restrict shipping

WIS.
IOWA
MICH.
PA.
NEB.
ILL.
IND.
OHIO
Gettysburg
Washington, D.C.
KANS.
MO.
VA.
Richmond
KY.
TENN.
N.C.
S.C.
Atlanta
GA.
ALA.
Vicksburg
MISS.
TEXAS
LA.
New Orleans
FLA.

Missouri R.
Mississippi R.
Ohio R.
ARK.

ATLANTIC
OCEAN

Gulf of Mexico

The Union

The Confederacy

Border states

Union strategy

Confederate strategy

0   400 Miles
0   400 Kilometers

HarperCollins Publishers © 1991

TOPIC 17
Overview of Civil War Strategy

BACKGROUND

Nearly every textbook in American history includes at least one battle map of the Civil War. However, the best place to start a study of the military aspects of that epic conflict is not with specific engagements, but with a map that outlines the overall strategy on both sides.

Note that some explanatory text is given on this map. These major points might be likened to headings on an outline with major campaigns and battles as subdivisions under each section.

PLACES

1. The border states were important to the development of strategy on both sides. Border states were those that remained in the Union, but where slavery was legal. Color the border states: Missouri, Kentucky, Maryland, Delaware, and (later) West Virginia.

2. The broad arrows indicating the thrust of the various military drives lend a dynamic quality to the map. The success of the Union advance down the Mississippi River was achieved with the fall of Vicksburg on July 4, 1863. Record the date on the map.

3. The basic Confederate strategy was to maintain several major armies in the field and to defend most of its territory. Grant's success in the West may have helped induce Lee to shift gears and to advance into Pennsylvania. If successful, Lee's move would demoralize the North and threaten Washington, D.C. Gettysburg (July 1–3, 1863) was the major battle in this campaign. It spelled the end of Confederate offensive moves. Date it on the map. Note that it was simultaneous with the siege of Vicksburg.

4. A basic element of Union strategy was a naval blockade that would intercept war materials bound for the Confederacy and prevent southern exports from being sold abroad. Draw a bold line on the map to indicate this blockade.

5. A second swath was cut through the Confederacy in a campaign that led southeast from the Ohio Valley. A series of battles around Chattanooga, Tennessee in late 1863 led to the capture of Atlanta in September 1864. From there, Sherman marched to the sea. Mark this route from Chattanooga to Savannah on the map with a broad arrow.

6. Grant's last campaign, in Virginia, kept punching at Lee's army from June 1864 until the surrender at Appomattox Court House on April 9, 1865. Label this site on the map, as well as Fort Sumpter, where the first shot was fired.

CIVIL WAR GEOGRAPHY

1. _____ Capitol of the Confederacy

2. _____ Border state surrounding Union capitol city

3. _____ Confederate stronghold on the Mississippi River

4. _____ State where the first shot of the Civil War was fired

5. _____ Where Lee surrendered

6. _____ Battle that stopped Lee's invasion of the North

7. _____ A border state west of the Mississippi River

8. _____ Month and year marking the key turning point of the Civil War

9. _____ True or false: The major troop movements of the Civil War tended to follow north-south routes rather than the traditional east-west transportation corridors.

10. _____ Remained loyal to the Union and became a state in 1863

1770

1780

1790

1800

1810

1820

1830

1840

1850

1860

1870

HarperCollins Publishers © 1991

TOPIC 18
The Young Nation: A Chronological Context, 1783–1865

BACKGROUND

The Peace of Paris in 1783 recognized the independence of the United States. The end of the Civil War in 1865 established the fact that the federal union was indeed an American nation. The two events are part of one historical process. The long lifetime that separated them witnessed many remarkable changes. A small nation of 3 million people clustered along the Atlantic seaboard was transformed into a continental empire embracing a population ten times as large.

This timeline helps you keep the major events in diachronic order, telling a story about building a modern nation. Using the right-hand side of the chart to record significant milestones in social, cultural, and economic history will help you develop some sense of the synchronic dimension of the time.

WORKING WITH TIME

1. Label the left-hand side of the chart "Political Events" and the right-hand side "Cultural and Economic Events."
2. The following years are often used as major turning points during the period. Identify the event and record it on your timeline. All of these happenings are political in nature.

   a. 1776 _____
   b. 1783 _____
   c. 1789 _____
   d. 1800 _____
   e. 1816 _____
   f. 1828 _____
   g. 1844 _____
   h. 1850 _____
   i. 1861 _____
   j. 1865 _____

3. Next record the following notable events from social and cultural history on the right-hand side of the page:

   1769   American Philosophical Society founded
   1793   Cotton gin invented
   1800   Weems's *Life of Washington*
   1807   Fulton's steamboat
   1813   First U.S. textile factory, Walthan, Massachusetts
   1820   Erie Canal completed
   1828   Baltimore and Ohio Railroad started
   1831   McCormick's reaper patented
   1836   First McGuffey reader
   1841   Brook Farm founded
   1848   Seneca Falls Convention
   1851   *Moby Dick*
   1852   *Uncle Tom's Cabin*
   1854   *Walden*
   1855   *Leaves of Grass*
   1862   Union Pacific charter
   1866   First elevated railroad, New York City

EXTENSIONS

Compose a letter supposedly written by an American at the end of any decade covered by this chart. In the letter review the major political, cultural, and economic events of the past ten years. Make some suggestions about how they are related. Begin by imagining the author and the person receiving the letter; then establish the setting in time and place.

HarperCollins Publishers © 1991

TOPIC 19
Atlanta: City of the New South, 1871

BACKGROUND

The rebuilding of Atlanta began as soon as the war ended. In 1868 the state capital was moved to Atlanta and two years later, when this view was published, the city's population exceeded 20,000. This was small by northern standards but marked the emergence of Atlanta as a leading city of the New South. The next year streetcars were introduced, a public school system was established, and the city solidified its position as the rail center of the southeast. By 1881 it celebrated its achievement in the International Cotton Exposition, a showcase for New South ideas.

The phrase "New South" does not really refer to a particular place or even to a specific period. It was, as C. Vann Woodward has observed, more a rallying cry or a slogan. "It vaguely set apart those whose faith lay in the future from those whose heart was with the past. . . ." (*Origins of the New South*, 1951, p. ix).

In this bird's eye view, Atlanta is pictured as a city looking to the future. The scene is the central portion of Albert Ruger's lithograph, which was published in St. Louis.

PLACES

1. Atlanta was founded by the Western and Atlantic Railroad in 1837. Originally known as Terminus, it soon became a rail center rather than the end of the line. General Sherman recognized its importance and so did investors after the Civil War. Two large roundhouses flank the railroad corridor that served to orient the town. At the center, along Alabama Street, was the new Union Depot. Label these railroad buildings.

2. Atlanta was also a governmental center, but the official buildings were pushed to the edge of the central business district. The city hall was the structure in a park at the very bottom of the view west of the roundhouse. The state house in 1871 looked like a business block. It is on Marietta Street just below the final "a" in Marietta. Label the State House and the City Hall.

3. The road pattern of Atlanta centered in the Five Points District just to the north of the depot, near the state house. Here roads extended to five key points including the towns of Marietta and Decatur, the popular Whitehall Tavern just out of town, and Standing Peachtree, a large Cherokee Nation town on the Chattahoochee River.

4. A dozen churches are evident on this view, most of them Methodist or Baptist congregations. The Roman Catholic house of worship is the one with twin steeples near City Hall. Highlight the various churches with a yellow color.

5. Four different railroads served Atlanta in 1871 and each had a freight house and other buildings scattered along the tracks. The Macon and Western Railroad's offices occupied the structure at the far left. The Georgia Railroad had its facilities at the lower right. Color all the railroad tracks on the page.

6. The largest building in the view was the Kimball House, a hotel next to Union Depot. Label it.

EXTENSIONS

Write an editorial for an Atlanta newspaper praising the accomplishments of the city in the last six years and setting out a New South agenda for continued growth and development. Refer to as many features on this view as possible.

HarperCollins Publishers © 1991

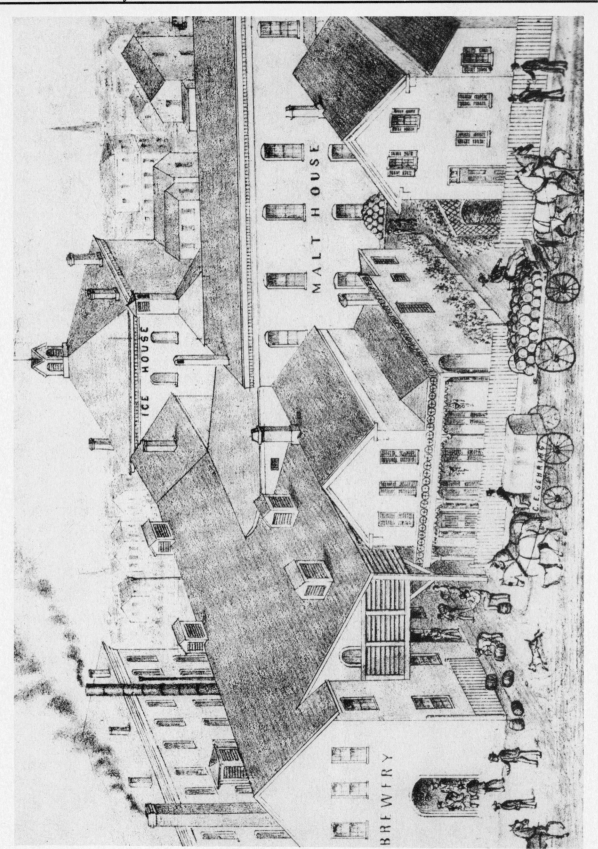

TOPIC 20
A Cleveland Brewery, 1874

BACKGROUND

This view of a Cleveland brewery in 1874 opens the door to a whole world of urban life, work, and culture. Unlike the standard pictures of breweries placed on boxes, labels, posters, and advertisements, this view does not picture the buildings in isolation. Instead, it shows the industrial buildings in the context of the city, right in the midst of a residential neighborhood.

C. E. Gehring's Brewery thus helps us picture the land uses existing side by side in 19-century cities. The first stage of urban development, the walking era, encouraged a mixture of residences, stores, factories, and institutional buildings as an efficient use of space. The streetcars that arrived after mid-century started the city on the process of sorting itself out into residential, commercial, industrial, and institutional districts. This had not yet occurred in 1874 at the corner of Pearl Road and Freeman Avenue just across the Cuyahoga River from downtown Cleveland.

OBSERVING THE CITYSCAPE

1. The complex of buildings making up Gehring's establishment included the _____ and the _____ in addition to the brewery itself. These were arranged around the residence and seem to interlock with neighboring structures. Color the three brewery structures red or brown.

2. The Gehring house and the one next door both suggest the _____ style in their pediments, but the original structures have been remodeled with additions and the use of more up-to-date decorations. Color the houses blue with white picket fences.

3. The street scene in the foreground is a flurry of activity as wagons come and go. Men are rolling barrels and a gentleman in his carriage proceeds past people engaged in serious _____ . Use color to reflect the liveliness of the street scene.

4. The labels on the three brewery buildings were probably added to the lithograph to help the reader observe the scene. Does their arrangement suggest a vertical or a horizontal flow in the production process? _____

5. The cityscape in the background presents a horizontal appearance with all of the buildings reaching about the same height except for _____ that punctuate the horizon.

6. The city is laid out on a gridiron plan that arranges all the buildings in neat rows with an orderly appearance. The only details that seem to be outside of the grid are _____ coming from the chimneys and the path of the _____ running in front of the wagon.

7. The smoke pouring from the chimneys of the brewery was a _____ of progress and prosperity. It highlighted the most important _____ in the scene. The brewery has numerous roof _____ to cool the building.

8. The ice house and the malt house seem to be more decorative in their architecture. Both have dentated _____ , and the former has a _____ . The flag flying proudly above it is probably a figment of the artist's imagination.

9. The beer wagon leaving the brewery probably will make regular stops at various _____ . There the _____ will be tapped and the beer dispensed for consumption at the bar or taken home in _____ .

10. The wagon returning to the brewery, labeled "_____ ," was probably an ice wagon.

Sources of Immigration, 1820–1919

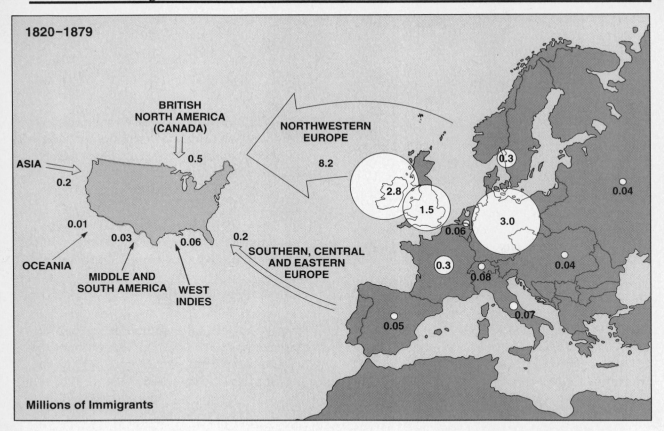

1820–1879

ASIA
0.2

BRITISH NORTH AMERICA (CANADA)
0.5

NORTHWESTERN EUROPE
8.2

0.3

0.04

2.8

1.5

3.0

0.06

0.01

0.03

0.06

0.3

0.04

OCEANIA

MIDDLE AND SOUTH AMERICA

WEST INDIES

0.2

SOUTHERN, CENTRAL AND EASTERN EUROPE

0.08

0.07

0.05

Millions of Immigrants

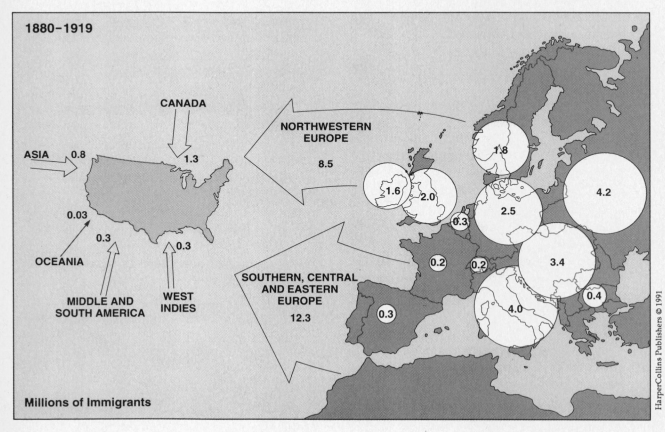

1880–1919

ASIA
0.8

CANADA
1.3

NORTHWESTERN EUROPE
8.5

1.8

4.2

1.6

2.0

0.3

2.5

0.03

0.3

0.2

0.2

3.4

OCEANIA

0.3

WEST INDIES

0.4

MIDDLE AND SOUTH AMERICA

SOUTHERN, CENTRAL AND EASTERN EUROPE
12.3

0.3

Millions of Immigrants

HarperCollins Publishers © 1991

42

TOPIC 21
Sources of Immigration, 1820–1919

BACKGROUND

American history is in large measure a story of people coming from other places to form new communities or to participate someway in the development of new societies. Each person who immigrated or migrated had his or her own special set of goals and experiences. Yet there were also many commonalities. The United States was a nation of newcomers.

Time, of course, was an important factor in understanding many similarities and differences in the immigrant experience. The two maps used here attempt to roughly quantify one aspect of this temporal difference, a contrast that is often made between the "old immigration" of the first part of the 19th century and the "new immigration" after 1880.

INTERPRETING A CARTOGRAM

1. The relative size of the circles and arrows on the maps is roughly equivalent to the number of immigrants involved. For example, between 1820 and 1879 _____ million immigrants from Germany arrived in the United States compared to _____ hundred thousand newcomers from France. The circle for Germans is thus about _____ times the area of the one for French immigrants.

2. The total number of immigrants was much greater for the new immigration in every large geographical category indicated on the map.

The only countries to show an absolute decline in numbers in the period after 1879 are _____, _____, and _____.

3. The bulk of the old immigrants came from three countries: _____, _____, and _____. Each of these continued to send many people to the Americas after 1879, but they were overshadowed by the migration from _____ and the _____ and _____ Empires.

4. The number of people coming to the United States from Asian places of origin increased _____ fold from the old to the new immigration.

5. The maps show that people entered the United States from _____ directions during _____ major periods of 19th-century immigration.

EXTENSIONS

Personalize one of these maps by recording the route taken either by your family or by that of one of your friends or acquaintances. Write a brief description of the experience using four headings: Decision to Leave, Experiences on the Journey, Choosing a New Home, Adjusting to a New Land.

HarperCollins Publishers © 1991

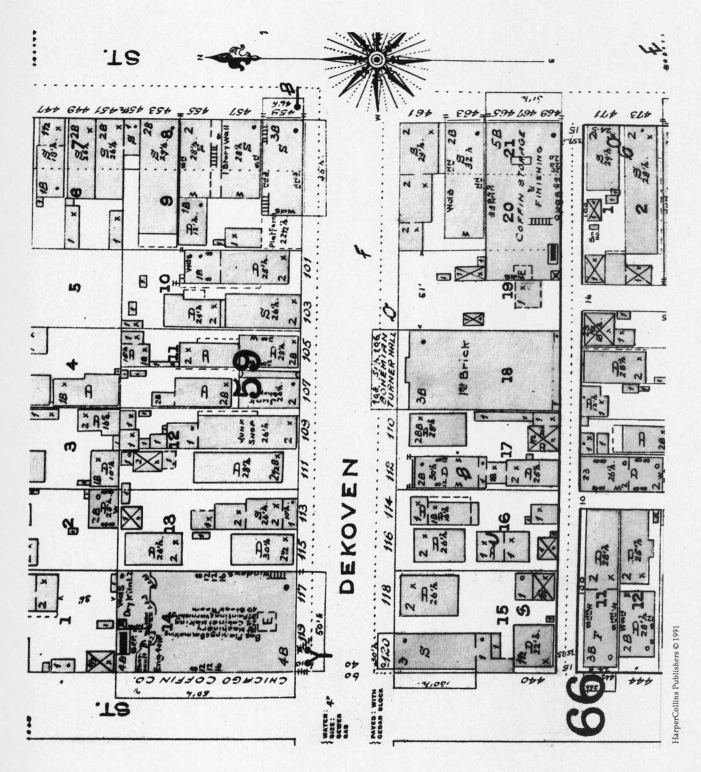

TOPIC 22
DeKoven Street, 1891

BACKGROUND

One function of history is to make it possible for the present generation to see how people lived in another age. Maps are an important tool for recreating the physical environment of bygone days—the landscapes and cityscapes of the past. Fire insurance maps produced during the second half of the 19th century are widely used sources for this purpose. This one is from Charles Rascher, *Atlas of Chicago*, I (1891). Similar maps are available for hundreds of cities and towns.

Fire insurance maps were made to help underwriters and agents assess the risk involved for a particular structure and to set an appropriate premium. A map of this nature is often called a Sanborn map after the name of a large national firm that produced insurance maps.

A wealth of detail on individual buildings and the urban environment is provided here, but a special key is needed to understand all the symbols. The maps provide information on the materials used in construction, the type of roof, the number of windows, the location of fire hydrants, the size of the water mains, the height of ceilings and buildings, the location of stairways, and so on.

WORKING WITH SPACE

1. Historians are often more interested in the nature of the streetscape than in any one individual building. This map portrays a walking city block, which typically has a mixed land use.

   a. *Industrial use.* Note the _____ factory at the northeast corner of Clinton and DeKoven streets (lot 14) and also at the southwest corner of Canal and DeKoven streets (lots 20 and 21).

   b. *Institutional use.* The _____ _____ Hall is in the middle of the block on the south side.

   c. *Commercial use.* All of the buildings marked with an "S" contain stores. Two _____ _____ are located across the street from the Turner Hall.

d. *Residential use.* Every building on this block except the coffin factory contained residences. "D" indicates a structure used only for dwelling purposes.

2. The coffin factory was located in two separate buildings at opposite ends of the block. The coffins were constructed at the west end, then wheeled down the street to be finished and stored in the other building where sawdust would not be a problem. It must have made for a "lively" street scene! Draw a line with an arrow to indicate the route of the coffins from the manufacturing to the finishing facility. The arrow points to the _____ (direction).

3. Buildings marked with an "X" were used as stables, mainly for horses. Other small buildings were woodsheds, outhouses, and the like. How many stables were located on the lot numbered 19? _____

4. The scene on DeKoven Street changed at different times of the day and week as different groups of people used it for different purposes.

   Note that the block on the south side of DeKoven Street had an alley but the one to the north did not. How wide was this alley? _____ feet.

5. The street numbers for each building are given on the street at the front. The odd numbers designated the _____ side of an east-west street while the even numbers were used on the _____ side.

EXTENSIONS

What does this map suggest about the people who lived on DeKoven Street—their social and economic class, ethnic origins, their hopes and fears? Write a commentary on this map describing the DeKoven Street neighborhood, its people, its spatial arrangements, and its time.

HarperCollins Publishers © 1991

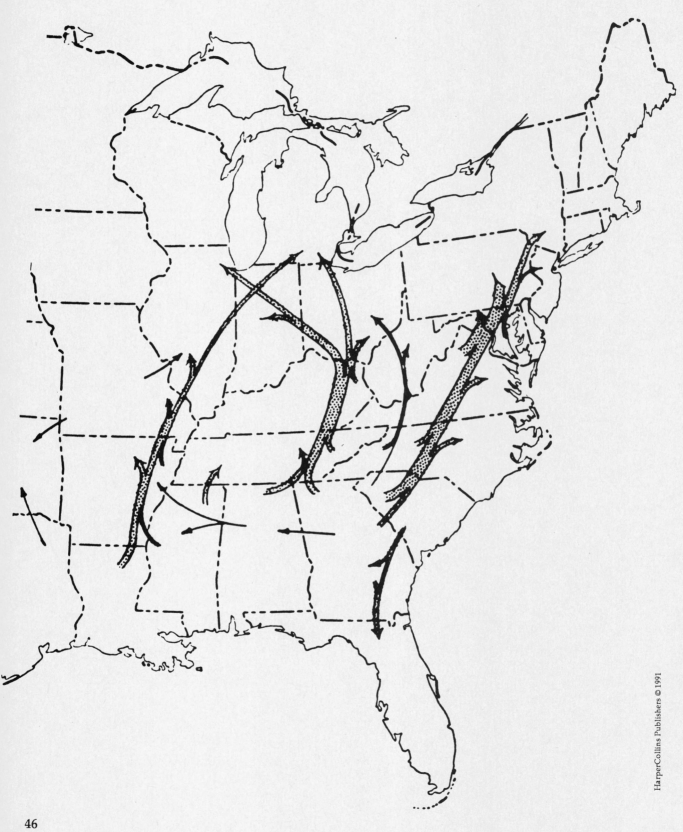

TOPIC 23
African-American Migration, 1865–1930

BACKGROUND

This map of African-American migration between the Civil War and the Great Depression is largely based on census data. It shows the net migration from one state to each of the others over this 65-year period. Minor flows are omitted and the larger ones are grouped together in arrows to give a graphic portrayal of the movement.

Note that the arrows are a form of graph since they are drawn according to a scale. This map is adapted from one in a report by the National Resources Commission which was, in turn, based on a study by Carter Goodrich, *et al.*, *Migration and Economic Opportunity* (1938).

The arrows simply locate the state of destination; they do not point to particular locations within each state. The use of graphs and charts like this became common with the rise of the social sciences in the late 19th and early 20th centuries. Authorities were convinced that the gathering of statistics and their careful plotting would lead to insights into social behavior.

PLACES

Label the following places on the map: Washington, D.C.; Tuskegee, Alabama; Atlanta; Niagara Falls, Canada; Harlem; New Orleans; Chicago; Philadelphia; Detroit; and New York City.

WORKING WITH SPACE

1. World War I was the most intensive period of African-American migration from the South to the North. The demand for labor increased with mobilization. As men left to serve in the Armed Forces, their jobs were sometimes filled by newcomers from the South. All of the states of Old Northwest except _____ received large numbers of migrating African Americans.

2. Movement to the North was often referred to as "the great exodus." Most of the migrants used railroads to reach northern cities. The Illinois Central and the Southern were the major north-south railroads at the time. Both started at New Orleans. The IC proceeded due north to Chicago while the Southern connected Birmingham, Alabama; Atlanta, Georgia; Greenville, South Carolina; Charlotte, North Carolina; Charlottesville, Virginia; and Washington, D. C. Draw these routes on the map and label them. Note that _____ , the eastern region least affected by the exodus, was most remote from these railroads.

3. The major routes suggested by the map were along the _____ River, across the Ohio gateway, and through the Great Valley of the _____ Mountains.

4. In the East the city of _____ seemed to be a major portal for the movement from the South to the North.

5. An interesting counter movement southward is evident as people from South Carolina and Georgia relocated in _____ .

EXTENSIONS

Use the library to find a primary source that documents the life and activities of African Americans during this period. Compose a brief essay explicating the document and connecting it to this map.

1870

1875

1880

1885

1890

1895

1900

1905

1910

1915

1920

HarperCollins Publishers © 1991

TOPIC 24

A Chronological Context for the Emergence of Modern America, 1870–1920

BACKGROUND

The left side of the chart will record significant events in the economic development of the nation and may be labeled "The Industrial Revolution in America." The right-hand side will be used for social and cultural events that suggest various responses to industrialization. Label this side "Responses to Industrialism."

WORKING WITH TIME

The chronology listed at the right suggests 23 significant dates that might be used to develop a narrative describing the American experience between 1870 and 1920. Events referring to the Industrial Revolution in America belong on one side of the page and the response to industrialism belongs on the other. Decide which events should go on each side and record them in their proper places. No set of events can be really considered the "correct" one, but a sample list is given in the answer section of the Appendix. Use the line before each date to record an "I" or an "R" to indicate which side of the chart would be most appropriate for each event.

	1869	Golden Spike
_____	1869	Golden Spike
_____	1873	Comstock Lode
_____	1876	Invention of the telephone
_____	1879	Standard Oil Trust
_____	1879	Knights of Labor founded
_____	1883	Brooklyn Bridge completed
_____	1886	Haymarket Riot
_____	1887	Interstate Commerce Act
_____	1888	Edward Bellamy, *Looking Backward*
_____	1889	Hull House founded
_____	1890	Sherman Antitrust Act
_____	1892	Populist Platform
_____	1894	Pullman Strike
_____	1895	Gasoline motor perfected
_____	1901	U.S. Steel Corporation
_____	1902	Great Coal Strike
_____	1906	*The Jungle*
_____	1908	Model T design
_____	1909	Great White Fleet
_____	1912	New Nationalism and New Freedom
_____	1913	Federal Reserve Act
_____	1916	Federal Highway Act
_____	1920	19th Amendment—Women's suffrage

HarperCollins Publishers © 1991

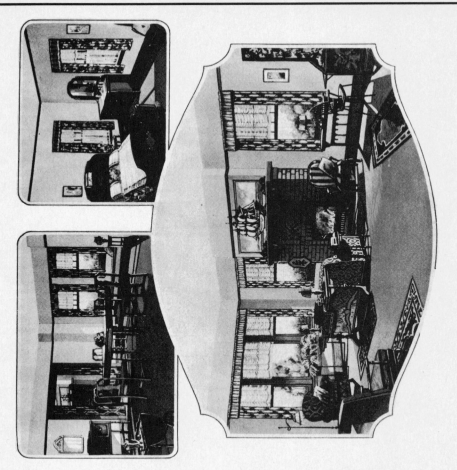

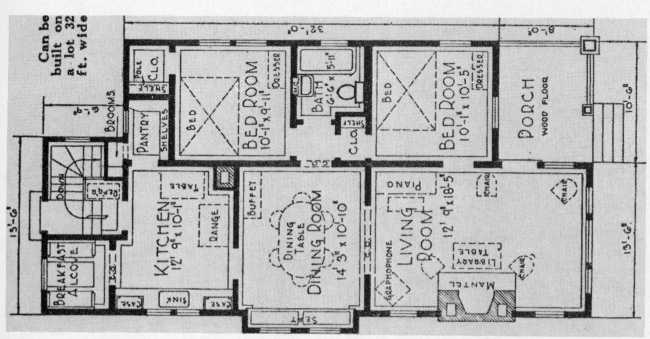

TOPIC 25
A Sears House of the 1920s

BACKGROUND

The most accurate mental maps we carry around in our heads are those of our houses. Yet we seldom think of a real map of our residence except when we are considering buying a new one. Floor plans have been standard features of home-building magazines and catalogues for over a 100 years. They furnish the historian with a rich source of information. The plans often reflect the life-style, technology, economy, attitudes, and the very spirit of the age in which the houses were built.

WORKING WITH SPACE

1. The plans and materials for the construction of this house were supplied by Sears, Roebuck and Company. A contractor then erected the building on the owner's lot and foundation. This bungalow was designed for a lot as narrow as _____ feet. The house itself was _____ feet wide.

2. Note how the entry to the house was indirect. The front door was difficult to see from the street. The wooden _____ served as a transition space between the public and private areas.

3. Upon entering the house a visitor would immediately see the fireplace, which served as the focal point of the living room. In addition to chairs, three other items suggest how this room

was to be used: _____ , _____ , and _____ . What type of records were current at this time? _____

4. Two doors led out of the living room into two distinct spaces in the house, one for sleeping and one for eating. Although the front bedroom is larger, the back bedroom has a more convenient closet arrangement. Which would you prefer? Note that only one dresser would fit in each room. What does this suggest about the amount of clothing each person had in the 1920s? _____ .

5. The food and eating space contains four separate areas: the _____ for formal meals, the _____ for food preparation, the _____ for informal dining, and the _____ for storing food and utensils. Note that the _____ is located in the back stairway in the traditional spot for an ice box.

EXTENSIONS

If you were to live in this house today, how would you remodel it to make it more convenient for contemporary needs? Write a proposal for this rehab job, staying within the limitation of the 32-foot lot. Include sketches and floor plans with your proposal.

By rail

By air

New York City

12 hours

1 day

12 hours

1 day

2 days

1 day

2 days

1 day

3 days

3 days

3 days

36 hours

400 Miles

200

400 Kilometers

200

0

0

TOPIC 26
Rates of Travel, 1930

BACKGROUND

In 1930 commercial air service was still in its infancy and railroads had passed the peak of their dominance in America's transportation network. This map starts in New York City and then connects all the points that are equidistant from it in regular time-distance intervals. The solid lines show the places that could be reached in the specified amount of time by railroads. The dotted lines provide similar data for air service. Lines like these on maps that connect points at which a variable has a constant value are called isopleths.

WORKING WITH SPACE

1. Note that the isopleths indicating the time-distance for railroads are given in units of _____ while those for airplanes are given in units of _____.

2. According to this map all the major cities on the Pacific coast could be reached by air from New York within _____ hours.

3. The most accessible Pacific Coast city from New York by rail was _____.

4. The city farthest west that could be reached within 12 hours from New York was _____, the capital of _____.

PLACES

Label the following cities on your map. Each was one of the nation's 20 largest cities in 1930.

1. San Francisco, the only one to be more than three days by rail from New York.

2. Kansas City, the only one to be located between the Mississippi River and the Pacific Ocean.

3. Boston, the only one to serve as the capital of its state.

4. New Orleans, the only one except Los Angeles to be located south of the mouth of the Ohio River.

5. Minneapolis, the only one to be located closer to the North Pole than to the equator.

6. Washington, the only one not located in a state.

7. St. Louis, the only Mississippi River city to be within a day's railroad trip of New York City.

8. Draw a rectangle on the map with Boston, Washington, St. Louis, and Minneapolis at the corners. Label it the "Manufacturing Belt." It contained 16 of the nation's 20 largest cities in 1930.

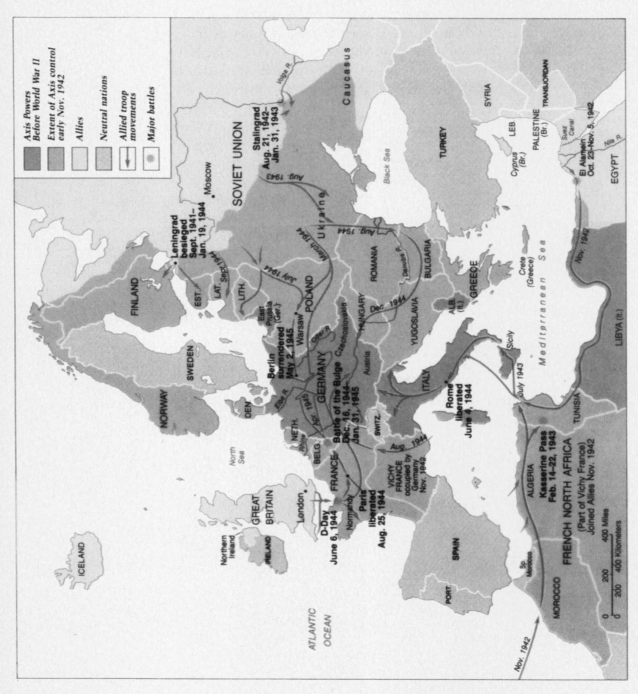

HarperCollins Publishers © 1991

TOPIC 27
World War II in Europe and North Africa

BACKGROUND

To follow the course of action in World War II, as millions of Americans did each day between 1941 and 1945, was to receive an extensive education in geography. In 1940 hardly any Americans could locate Kasserine Pass, Corregidor, Anzio, and Hiroshima, places that became reference points in everyday conversation a few years later. To study World War II today, it is necessary to relearn the location of key places and the routes taken by military forces.

PLACES

1. This is a complex map. The best place to start an exposition of it is by noting the date of its base, November 1942, at the high tide of Axis expansion in Europe and North Africa. Draw a bold line indicating the territory controlled by the Axis powers this time.

2. Highlight the nations that were neutral in World War II: Sweden, Ireland, Switzerland, Turkey, Portugal, and Spain.

3. The lines and arrows trace Allied troop movements as they liberated the conquered territory and invaded the Axis nations. Reference dates for key battles help fit the action together in proper sequence. Place the following events in chronological order, indicating **A** for the earliest, **B** for the next, and so on. Then place each letter on the map in the proper location:

   _____ Normandy invasion

   _____ Kasserine Pass

   _____ Stalingrad siege begins

   _____ Liberation of Rome

   _____ Surrender of Berlin

   _____ Battle of the Bulge

4. France was occupied by Germany in November 1942, when an accommodation with the enemy was reached by the Vichy government. At the same time France's North African colonies officially joined the Allies and an Allied force landed in _____ on the Atlantic Ocean.

5. D–Day, the code name for the _____ invasion, was _____ , 1944. It was scheduled to occur after the Axis Forces had been pushed back in the "soft underbelly" of Europe. Rome was liberated on _____ , _____ days before D–Day.

EXTENSIONS

Using this map, describe the action in the European theater of World War II between November 1942 and May 1945. Before this date the Axis powers won a long series of battles. Then the tide turned. You could describe each year's events in a separate paragraph.

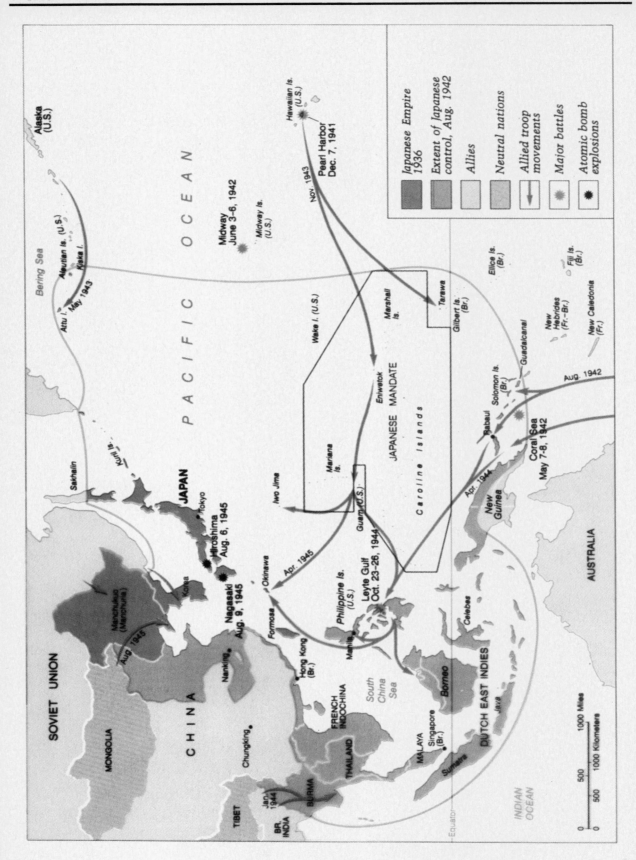

Japanese Empire 1936

Extent of Japanese control, Aug. 1942

Allies

Neutral nations

Allied troop movements

Major battles

Atomic bomb explosions

Alaska (U.S.)

Bering Sea

Aleutian Is. (U.S.)

Attu I. May 1943

Kiska I.

Kuril Is.

Sakhalin

SOVIET UNION

MONGOLIA

Manchukuo (Manchuria)

Aug. 1945

TIBET

BR. INDIA

BURMA

Jan. 1944

THAILAND

FRENCH INDOCHINA

Chungking

CHINA

Nanking

Hong Kong (Br.)

MALAYA

Singapore (Br.)

Sumatra

South China Sea

Borneo

Celebes

Java

DUTCH EAST INDIES

JAPAN

Tokyo

Hiroshima Aug. 6, 1945

Nagasaki Aug. 9, 1945

Korea

Formosa

Okinawa

Apr. 1945

Philippine Is. (U.S.)

Manila

Leyte Gulf Oct. 23-26, 1944

Apr. 1945

Guam (U.S.)

Iwo Jima

Mariana Is.

JAPANESE MANDATE

Caroline Islands

Eniwetok

Wake I. (U.S.)

Marshall Is.

Tarawa

Gilbert Is. (Br.)

PACIFIC OCEAN

Midway June 3-6, 1942

Midway Is. (U.S.)

Nov 1943

Pearl Harbor Dec. 7, 1941

Hawaiian Is. (U.S.)

Ellice Is. (Br.)

New Hebrides (Fr.-Br.)

Fiji Is. (Br.)

New Caledonia (Fr.)

Guadalcanal

Solomon Is.

Rabaul

Apr. 1944

Aug. 1942

New Guinea

Coral Sea May 7-8, 1942

AUSTRALIA

INDIAN OCEAN

Equator

0   500   1000 Miles

0   500   1000 Kilometers

HarperCollins Publishers © 1991

TOPIC 28
World War II in the Pacific

BACKGROUND

In one way this map of the Pacific in World War II resembles the preceding Atlantic theater map. It shows the farthest extent of control by Japanese forces and then the Allied invasion routes by which the conquered regions were won back. The obvious difference, however, is that the European map featured land battles while the Pacific map records mostly battles at sea.

PLACES

1. The base map used for this topic has several unusual characteristics. Most of the space is devoted to the Pacific Ocean, but the map extends eastward only to the Hawaiian Islands. Thus, although the map establishes the relationship between the Aleutian Islands and Australia, that between Asia and the west coast of North America must be formed from memory. Circle the Hawaiian Islands.

2. The equator is the only grid line on the map. Meridians would run perpendicular to the equator, providing a map with true directions but greatly exaggerating area and distance in the high latitudes. In reality, the island of Java is almost twice the size of the island of Sakhalin. Circle Sakhalin and Java and label the equator.

3. Note the Pacific Islands mandated to Japan by the League of Nations. These were "class C" mandates, which could be annexed by Japan. Shade this area in the Pacific.

4. In 1910 Japan annexed Korea and in the 1930s it realized a long-time objective by occupying Manchuria. Later it extended its influence to other parts of China. Circle Manchuria and Korea.

5. The outbreak of World War II in Europe provided Japan with the opportunity to seize the colonies of the warring nations in Southeast Asia. The United States, a noncombatant with its interest in the Philippines, was the only nation standing in the way. Circle the Philippine Islands.

6. Some historians believe Japan wanted to quickly establish the boundaries of its East Asian Co-Prosperity Sphere and then hang on to defend this territory while the Allies became exhausted in a long war. Draw a red line around the East Asian Co-Prosperity Sphere.

EXTENSIONS

Two great naval battles of 1942 turned the tide against the Japanese: Coral Sea and Midway Island. In both cases the battles were fought with carrier-based airplanes. The ships never got close enough to engage directly in combat with each other. Write a brief account of one of these battles. Try to include a map showing the the action in some detail.

HarperCollins Publishers © 1991

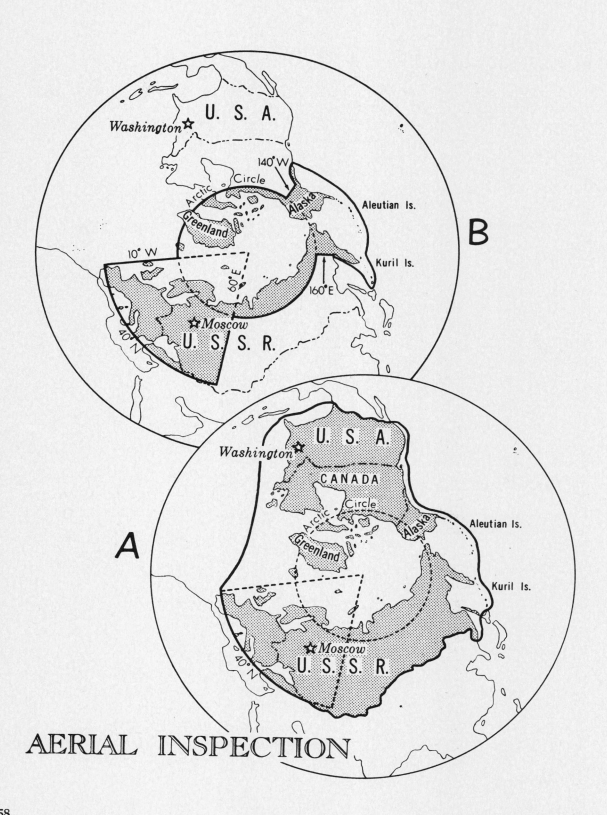

AERIAL INSPECTION

TOPIC 29
Open Skies in the Northern Hemisphere

BACKGROUND

Summit meetings between the President of the United States and the First Secretary of the Communist Party in the U.S.S.R. always were an occasion for Western journalists to take stock of the two blocs in the Cold War. How did they compare? Where were the trouble spots in the world in which their interests conflicted? How could tensions and confrontations be reduced? These questions often called for maps like Dwight D. Eisenhower's open skies proposal at the first summit on July 21, 1955.

This map by Robert C. Kingsbury is from *An Atlas of Soviet Affairs* (1965), one of a series of inexpensive atlases of the contemporary world published in the 1950s and 1960s by Frederick A. Praeger. The atlas included both Eisenhower's original 1955 proposal (map A) and an alternative plan suggested a few years later (map B). A polar projection is used to place the United States, the Soviet Union, and Europe into a close relationship with one another. The use of polar projections of the Northern Hemisphere became popular after World War II.

PLACES

Use map B to label some additional places on the map:

1. Oceans: Atlantic, Pacific, Arctic
2. Continents: North America, Europe, Asia, Africa.
3. National capitals: Ottawa, London, Paris, Peking, Tokyo.
4. Meridians: The Prime Meridian and the 180th Meridian.
5. Your home town.

WORKING WITH SPACE

Use map A to answer the following questions:

1. The center of this map is the _____.
2. Any straight line that begins at the center of this map proceeds in a _____ direction.
3. The wedge that looks like a slice of pie on the maps defined the proposed "denuclearized zones" of Europe. The denuclearized zones extended only to the _____ parallel.
4. Note the importance given to Europe on these maps. Both Prime Minister Anthony Eden of_____and _____ Premier Edgar Faure were full participants at Geneva.
5. The speed and range of the weapons at the time made the _____ a key line in respect to launching a surprise attack. The DEW (Distant Early Warning) facilities in North America were soon stationed along this line.

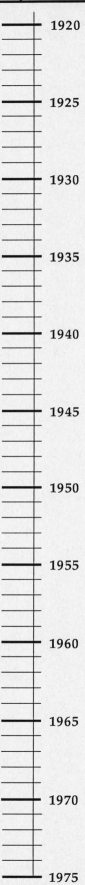

1920

1925

1930

1935

1940

1945

1950

1955

1960

1965

1970

1975

HarperCollins Publishers © 1991

TOPIC 30
A Chronological Context for 20th-Century America, 1920–1976

BACKGROUND

After World War I the student of American history is forced to keep two chronologies in mind, one centering on foreign events and the other tracing domestic affairs. Much of the dynamic quality of the American experience between World War I and the celebration of the Bicentennial of Independence in 1976 reflects the interaction between these two realms. There is also a dramatic movement over time as the mood of the nation in respect to foreign affairs shifted through three major stages. First there was a feeling that America could gain security by selectively isolating itself from the world at large. Then the force of events pulled the United States into another World War and it emerged as the dominant global power. Finally a new state of mind struggled to gain acceptance as the limits of American power and the frailties of its institutions were revealed in the days of Vietnam and Watergate.

WORKING WITH TIME:
Domestic Affairs

Use the left-hand side of the timeline to record the following events in domestic affairs. Be sure to place the heading at the top of this column.

1921	Sacco and Vanzetti case begins
1925	Scopes Trail
1927	Lindbergh's transatlantic flight
1929	Stock market crash
1933	New Deal legislation begins
1935	Neutrality Act
1939	"God Bless America" written
1946	Atomic Energy Commission
1949	Fair Deal proposals
1954	McCarthy hearings
1956	Montgomery bus boycott
1958	NASA founded

1964	Great Society legislation
1967	Summer of violence
1969	Moon landing
1970	Student protest movement at height
1972	Watergate break-in
1973	Energy crisis
1974	Nixon resignation

WORKING WITH TIME:
Foreign Events

Next record the following events on the right-hand side of the timeline. Label the column "Foreign Events."

1920	League of Nations established
1922	Mussolini takes power in Italy
1925	Hitler publishes *Mein Kampf*
1933	Nazi Revolution
1936	Pan American Congress
1938	Munich Conference
1940	German blitzkriegs, Battle of Britain
1941	Pearl Harbor
1945	Yalta Conference, UN Conference
1950–53	Korean War
1957	Sputnik
1959	Cuban Revolution
1962	Cuban Missile Crisis
1964–72	Vietnam War
1973	Fourth Arab–Israeli War

EXTENSIONS

Develop a list of five connections between domestic affairs and foreign events as suggested by this timeline. State your observations in complete sentences.

HarperCollins Publishers © 1991

ATLANTIC
OCEAN

YANKEE

Boston

EMPIRE

New York City

Baltimore

MID-ATLANTIC

Norfolk

CAROLINA

TROPICANA
(includes Puerto Rico and
the Virgin Islands)

Miami

Great Lakes

INDUSTRY

Detroit

Chicago

Atlanta

NEW SOUTH

NORTH
HEARTLAND

St.
Louis

SOUTH
HEARTLAND

GULF COAST

Houston

Gulf of Mexico

400 Miles

400 Kilometers

200

200

0

0

NORTH PLAINS

Minneapolis

CENTRAL
PLAINS

Kansas
City

SOUTH
PLAINS

Dallas

Denver

ROCKY

ANGELINA

PACIFICA

PACIFIC OCEAN

100 Miles

100 Kilometers

0

Los Angeles

PACIFICA

San
Francisco

PACIFIC
OCEAN

PACIFICA

Gulf of Alaska

400 Miles

400 Kilometers

0

0

BERING
SEA

PACIFIC
OCEAN

HarperCollins Publishers © 1991

TOPIC 31
Sixteen Regional States

BACKGROUND

This plan called for using 16 major cities as hubs for new regional states. Developed by Stanley D. Brunn in *Geography and Politics in America* (1974), it tried to balance economic, social, and cultural factors with political realities in the early 1970s.

PLACES

1. Three states would supply 6 of the 16 capitol cities for the proposed regional provinces. _____ and _____ , both California cities, would serve _____ and Pacifica respectively.

2. The two major cities in Missouri would also become hubs: _____ for the _____ and _____ for the _____ .

3. _____ and _____ would leave Texas to become centers of the _____ and the _____ .

4. Note that Indianapolis is near the boundary between four provinces _____ _____ , _____ _____ , _____ and _____ _____ .

5. _____ includes _____ and the _____ _____ but has its capital on the mainland in Miami.

6. _____ and _____ , former states, would become outlying parts of Pacifica in this proposal.

WORKING WITH SPACE

Note that Pennsylvania's large cities do not figure to become capitals in this proposal, yet Pennsylvania is often called the Keystone State. How can a state be considered so central in American history yet not form a focus for a new regional grouping?

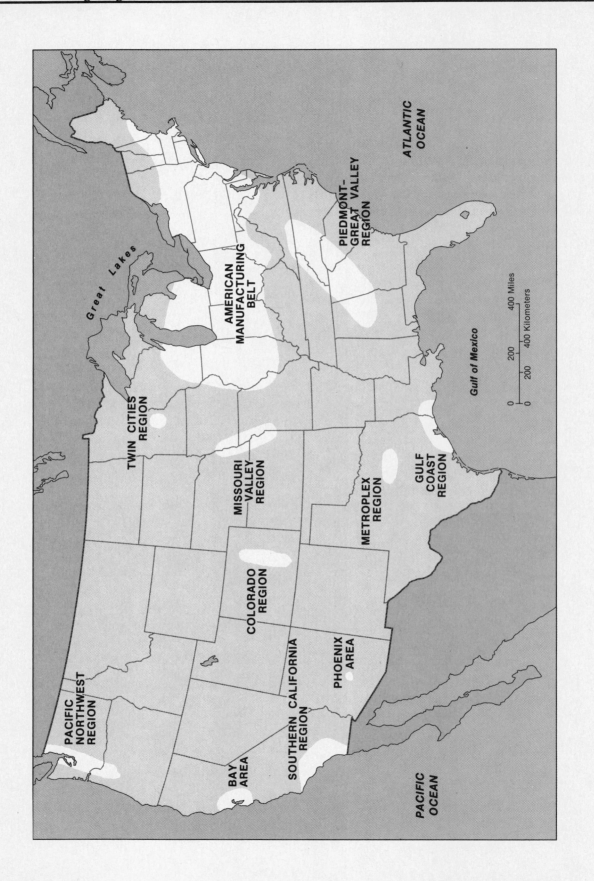

TOPIC 32
Manufacturing Regions, 1979

BACKGROUND

By 1979 the phrase "postindustrial society" was widely used to describe the United States. Yet industry remained at the core of the American economy. The index of national economic health was still measured each day by the Dow–Jones industrial average of selected, representative stock prices. One striking aspect of this map of the nation's manufacturing regions in 1979 is the dispersal of large-scale industrial activities in a variety of regions across the continent.

PLACES

1. The _____ _____ _____ stretched from southern New England west to Green Bay, and from Chesapeake Bay to the Mississippi River. It reached as far north as Lake Ontario and as far south as the Ohio River. This is the region where industrialization began and it remained the major factory region of the nation. Label Green Bay, Chesapeake Bay, the Ohio River, and the Mississippi River.

2. The _____ _____ _____ region of the upland South started as a textile producer and then branched out into a variety of industries. The complex, scattered in many small cities, had Atlanta as its major focus. Label Atlanta.

3. Texas had two important regions, both rapidly growing in 1979: the _____ and _____ _____ regions. Houston was the center of the petrochemical industry and Dallas–Ft. Worth anchored the upstate region. Label these cities.

4. A series of dispersed manufacturing centers centered on _____–St. Paul; Kansas City; Denver; Phoenix; and the Seattle–_____ corridor. Label these cities.

5. The _____ _____ in California was the center of the new high-technology electronics industry. Southern California had many advantages, one of which was a huge nearby market. Label the two major cities of Southern California: _____ and _____.

EXTENSIONS

Find out which firms were used to compile the Dow–Jones industrial average in 1979. Locate their headquarter cities on the map and label each company. Write a caption for the map explaining something about the geography behind industrial activity in America during 1979.

HarperCollins Publishers © 1991

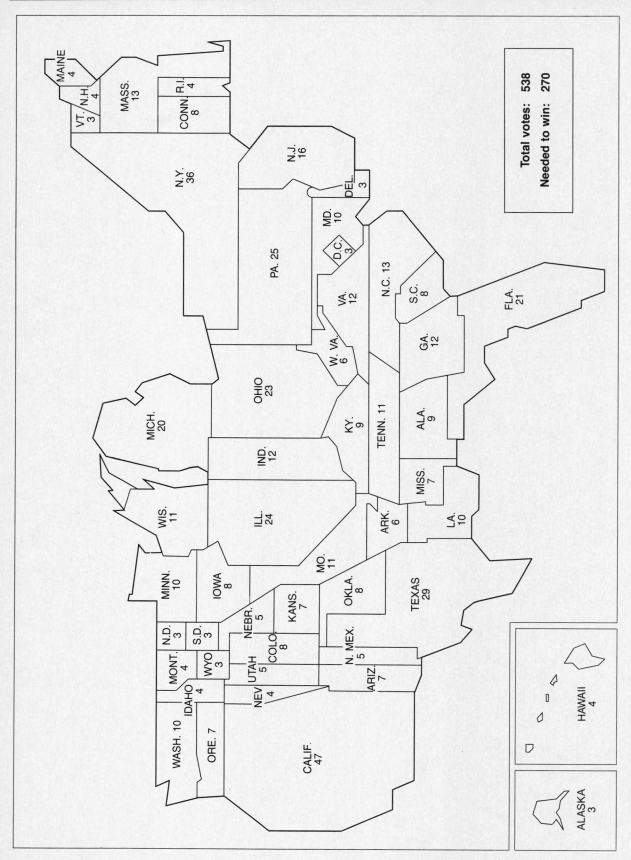

Total votes: 538
Needed to win: 270

MAINE
4

VT.
3
N.H.
4

MASS.
13

R.I.
4

CONN.
8

N.Y.
36

N.J.
16

DEL.
3

PA. 25

MD.
10

D.C.
3

VA.
12

N.C. 13

S.C.
8

FLA.
21

W. VA.
6

OHIO
23

KY.
9

TENN. 11

GA.
12

ALA.
9

MICH.
20

IND.
12

MISS.
7

LA.
10

WIS.
11

ILL.
24

ARK.
6

MINN.
10

IOWA
8

MO.
11

OKLA.
8

TEXAS
29

N.D.
3

S.D.
3

NEBR.
5

KANS.
7

MONT.
4

WYO.
3

COLO.
8

N. MEX.
5

IDAHO
4

UTAH
5

NEV.
4

ARIZ.
7

WASH. 10

ORE. 7

CALIF.
47

HAWAII
4

ALASKA
3

HarperCollins Publishers © 1991

TOPIC 33
The Electoral Vote in the 1980s

BACKGROUND

This map is really a form of a graph or a chart. It could be considered a graph if the area of each state were strictly proportional to its share of the electoral votes. An artist making a map like this often takes some liberties with the proportions to get the states into recognizable shapes and in their proper locations. The area of each state is shown in rough proportion to its number of electoral votes. It suggests the relative political power of each state in electing a president and in influencing congressional action.

THE ELECTORAL SYSTEM BEHIND THE MAP

1. In the 1980s there were _____ states with more than 20 electoral votes. _____ of them touched the Great Lakes; the other _____ were Sunbelt states. The total electoral votes in these large states was _____ , far short of the 270 needed to win an election.

2. The apportionment of representatives is determined on the basis of the _____ taken every _____ years. A new electoral map and new congressional districts are then created for each decade. The one exception was the 1920s, when Congress did not reapportion its members.

3. In 1929 Congress set a limit of 435 members in the House of Representatives. This was done by statute rather than by a Constitutional _____, which means that Congress could increase the number at any time.

4. Each state is guaranteed three votes in the Electoral College, one for its _____ and two for its _____.

5. In the 1980s there were six states with the minimum number of votes in the Electoral College. These were:

   New England: _____

   Mid Atlantic: _____

   Great Plains: _____

   _____

   Mountain West _____

   Far North: _____

EXTENSIONS

The governor of your home state is considering a run for the presidency in the next election. Develop a campaign strategy for his or her election. Use a map like this one to explain the plan and tabulate the winning electoral votes.

ATLANTIC OCEAN

Great Lakes

Gulf of Mexico

400 Miles
400 Kilometers
200
200
0
0

PACIFIC OCEAN

100 Miles
100 Kilometers
0

Gulf of Alaska

400 Miles
400 Kilometers
0

BERING SEA

PACIFIC OCEAN

TOPIC 34
Interstate Highways, 1980

BACKGROUND

The federal role in highway construction began in 1806 with funding for the Cumberland Road. During World War II Congress approved a plan for a system of interstate defense highways. Later it was decided to extend the new superhighways into the centers of the cities. The Federal Highway Trust Fund was set up in 1956 to pay 90 percent of the cost of construction.

Half of the system was in use by 1966. In 1980 the roads were almost finished. In many ways the highway pattern reproduced that of the railroads. Each state was served by at least one north-south and one east-west route. Alaska and Hawaii were not included in the original plans.

PLACES

Certain cities stand out as hubs on the highway network. Label the following:

Boston	Detroit
New York	Chicago
Harrisburg	Dallas
Atlanta	Oklahoma City
Columbia, S.C.	Kansas City
Indianapolis	Denver
St. Louis	Salt Lake City

WORKING WITH SPACE

1. The first major superhighway in the nation, the Pennsylvania Turnpike, was built between 1940 and 1951. It served the same function as the old Cumberland Road, except that it linked the Ohio River with the Delaware River rather than with the Potomac River. Mark the Pennsylvania Turnpike on the map. It connects the two major cities in Pennsylvania: _____ and _____.

2. One city that has benefited substantially from the interstate highway system is _____, the capital of Indiana.

3. Old U.S. Highway 66 between Chicago and Los Angeles was replaced by a series of interstate routes. Mark this major corridor on the map, beginning at Chicago and proceeding through St. Louis, Oklahoma City, Albuquerque, and Flagstaff to Los Angeles. In which state did U.S. 66 cross the continental divide?

_____

4. North-south routes in the interstate system have odd numbers; east-west routes are even numbered. Thus I80 crosses I29 in Omaha. Which route would a motorist at this point use to get to these cities, 80 or 29?

   _____ a. Des Moines

   _____ b. Kansas City

   _____ c. Fargo

   _____ d. Cheyenne

   _____ e. Toledo

5. Note that the interstate highways closely follow major rivers in a few cases: the _____ River by I84 in Oregon, the _____ River by I55 between Memphis and St. Louis, and the _____ River by I87 south of Albany, New York.

EXTENSIONS

A. The Avenue of the Saints is the name given to a proposed extension of the interstate highway system that would connect St. Louis and St. Paul–Minneapolis. Plan a specific route for this suggested highway and write a proposal listing the advantages of the route you have developed. Include a copy of this map explaining how the new route would fit into the overall interstate system. Present the proposal in the format of an article for the Sunday magazine supplement in a St. Louis or a St. Paul newspaper.

B. Write a letter to the editor of one of these newspapers opposing the project and advocating the improvement of existing highways.

1950

1955

1960

1965

1970

1975

1980

1985

1990

1995

2000

HarperCollins Publishers © 1991

TOPIC 35
A Chronological Context for My Lifetime

BACKGROUND

The contemporary period of American history is your lifetime. Use the timeline at the left or adapt it so that you can record the important events in your life on the left-hand side of the page. Title this personal chronology "My Life." Your birth date is the obvious place to begin, but feel free to record any events that are important to you. Make sure that you have at least ten items.

WORKING WITH TIME

On the other side of the sheet record at least 20 major events in American history during this period. Be sure to include both foreign and domestic events and listings referring to society, culture, and the economy in addition to political topics.

EXTENSIONS

Now you are in a position to write a preliminary sketch of your life informed by the historical context in which it has been lived. Write such a sketch trying to be as objective and as insightful as possible. You can include some maps to suggest the spatial context of your life as well.

If you want to extend this assignment into a large project, or if you need help in getting ideas, there are several helpful manuals on family history you can consult. Your librarian can help you find them. One of the best is *Your Family History: A Handbook for Research and Writing* by David E. Kyvig and Myron A. Marty (Arlington Heights, Illinois: AHM Publishing Company, 1978).

ANSWERS

TOPIC 1
A Global Quiz: **1.** F; **2.** T; **3.** T; **4.** T; **5.** T; **6.** T; **7.** F.

TOPIC 2
Working with Space: **1.** d; **2.** Antarctica; **3.** poles, South America, Africa, Amazon, Nile; **4.** 180°, 90° W, 90° E, 0°; **5.** Atlantic Ocean, Strait of Gibraltar, Mediterranean Sea, Suez Canal, Red Sea, Indian Ocean, Strait of Malacca, South China Sea, Pacific Ocean, Panama Canal, Caribbean Sea.

TOPIC 3
Working with Space: **1.** 15; **2.** Washington, Oregon, California; **3.** Humboldt, Great Salt.

TOPIC 7
Working with Space: **1.** F; **2.** B; **3.** G; **4.** E; **5.** A; **6.** D; **7.** C.

TOPIC 8
Places: **1.** France, Spain; **2.** Hudson River; **3.** Philadelphia; **4.** Virginia, Maryland; **5.** west; **6.** 1733; **7.** coastal plain, Appalachian, yes; **8.** Kentucky, Tennessee, Cincinnati, Louisville; **9.** west, north, south, Ohio; **10.** Ohio, Indiana.

TOPIC 9
Working with Space: **1.** T; **2.** T; **3.** F; **4.** F; **5.** T; **6.** T.

TOPIC 10
Quiz: **1.** did not; **2.** did; **3.** did; **4.** did; **5.** did not.

TOPIC 11
Places and dates: **1.** Lexington; **2.** Quebec; **3.** Howe evacuates Boston; **4.** New York; **5.** Trenton; **6.** Brandywine; **7.** Bemis Heights; **8.** Vincennes; **9.** Charleston; **10.** Cowpens; **11.** Guildford Courthouse; **12.** Yorktown.
Working with Space and Time: **1a.** Lexington, **b.** Yorktown; **2. a.** South, **b.** West, **c.** South, **d.** North; **3.** Quebec; **4.** Yorktown, October 19, 1781, Cornwallis, Lafayette; **5.** Virginia.

TOPIC 12
Working with Time: **4a.** T; **b.** T; **c.** T; **d.** T; **e.** F; **f.** T; **g.** T.

TOPIC 13
Capital Commentary: **1.** Pennsylvania; **2.** Georgetown, king; **3.** head of navigation; **4.** Virginia, Maryland; **5.** Eastern Branch.

TOPIC 14
Working with Space: **1.** Louisiana Purchase; **2.** Ohio, Indiana, Illinois; **3.** Louisiana, Mississippi, Alabama; **4.** Missouri; **5.** Louisiana, Florida, Michigan; **6.** Florida, Michigan; **6.** 49th, Vancouver; **7.** Rio Grande, Gadsden, 1853; **8.** Michigan, Florida, Wisconsin; **9.** Texas, third, half; **10.** California.

TOPIC 15
Working with Space: **1.** Ohio; **2.** Mississippi, Great Salt Lake, Pacific; **4.** Arkansas, Missouri; **5.** two.

TOPIC 17
Civil War Geography: **1.** Richmond; **2.** Maryland; **3.** Vicksburg; **4.** South Carolina; **5.** Appomattox Court House; **6.** Gettysburg; **7.** Missouri; **8.** July 1863; **9.** True; **10.** West Virginia.

TOPIC 18
Working with Time: **2a.** Declaration of Independence, **b.** Peace of Paris; **c.** Inauguration of Washington, **d.** Election of Jefferson begins the Republican Ascendancy, **e.** Election of Monroe begins the Era of Good Feelings, **f.** Election of Jackson ushers in the Age of the Common Man, **g.** Election of Polk and the triumph of Manifest Destiny, **h.** Compromise of 1850 begins the Road to War, **i.** Outbreak of the Civil War, **j.** End of the Civil War and the beginning of Reconstruction.

TOPIC 20
Observing the Cityscape: **1.** malt house, ice house; **2.** Greek Revival; **3.** conversation; **4.** horizontal; **5.** church steeples; **6.** smoke, dog; **7.** symbol, building, vents; **8.** cornices, cupola; **9.** saloons, barrels, growlers; **10.** C. E. Gehring.

TOPIC 21
Interpreting a Cartogram: **1.** three, three, ten; **2.** Ireland, Germany, France; **3.** Ireland, England, Germany, Italy, Austrian-Hungarian, Russian; **4.** four; **5.** four, both.

TOPIC 22
Working with Space: **1a.** Chicago Coffin, **b.** Bohemian Turner, **c.** junk shops; **2.** east; **3.** two; **4.** fifteen; **5.** north, south.

TOPIC 23
Places: **1.** Wisconsin; **2.** New England; **3.** Mississippi, Appalachian; **4.** Washington; **5.** Florida.

TOPIC 24
Industrial Revolution: 1869 Golden Spike; 1873 Comstock Lode; 1876 Invention of the telephone;1879 Standard Oil Trust; 1883 Brooklyn Bridge completed; 1895 Gasoline motor perfected; 1901 U.S. Steel Corporation; 1908 Model T design; 1909 Great White Fleet; 1913 Federal Reserve Act; 1916 Federal Highway Act.
Response to Industrialism: 1879 Knights of Labor founded; 1886 Haymarket Riot; 1887 Interstate Commerce Act; 1888 Edward Bellamy, *Looking Backward;* 1889 Hull House founded; 1890 Sherman Antitrust Act; 1892 Populist Platform; 1894 Pullman Strike; 1902 Great Coal Strike; 1906

HarperCollins Publishers © 1991

The Jungle; 1912 New Nationalism and New Freedom; 1920 19th Amendment—Women's Suffrage.

TOPIC 25
Working with Space: **1.** 32, 24; **2.** porch; **3.** library table, graphophone, piano, wax cylinders; **4.** The amount of clothing was very limited compared to today. Note that there is no separate closet for coats. **5.** dining room, kitchen, breakfast alcove, pantry, refrigerator.

TOPIC 26
Working with Space: **1.** days, hours; **2.** 36; **3.** Los Angeles; **4.** DesMoines, Iowa.

TOPIC 27
Places: **3A.** Stalingrad; **B.** Kasserine Pass; **C.** Liberation of Rome; **D.** Normandy; **E.** Battle of the Bulge; **F.** Surrender of Berlin; **4.** Morocco; **5.** Normandy, June 6, June 4, two.

TOPIC 29
Working with Space: **1.** North Pole; **2.** southerly; **3.** 40th; **4.** Great Britain, French; **5.** Arctic Circle.

TOPIC 31
Places: **1.** Los Angeles, San Francisco, Angelina; **2.** St. Louis, Southern Heartland, Kansas City, Central Plains; **3.** Dallas, Houston, South Plains, Gulf Coast; **4.** North Heartland, South Heartland, Industry, New South; **5.** Tropicana, Puerto Rico, Virgin Islands; **6.** Alaska, Hawaii.
Working with Space: A keystone is transitional in nature, receiving and balancing forces that are exerted in opposite directions. Thus Pennsylvania's transitional nature between North and South, East and West is confirmed by this proposal.

TOPIC 32
Places: **1.** American Manufacturing Belt; **2.** Piedmont-Great Valley; **3.** Metroplex, Gulf Coast; **4.** Minneapolis, Portland; **5.** Bay Area, Los Angeles, San Diego.

TOPIC 33
The Electoral System behind the Map: **1.** eight, five, three, 225; **2.** census, ten; **3.** amendment; **4.** representative, senators; **5.** Vermont, Delaware, North Dakota, South Dakota, Wyoming, Alaska.

TOPIC 34
Working with Space: **1.** Philadelphia, Pittsburgh; **2.** Indianapolis; **3.** New Mexico; **4a.** I80, **b.** I29, **c.** I 29, **d.** I80, **e.** I80; **5.** Columbia, Mississippi, Hudson.

HarperCollins Publishers © 1991

ARCTIC OCEAN

CANADA

UNITED STATES

MEXICO

Equator

Alaska

Hawaii

PACIFIC OCEAN

90° W

180°

NEW ZEALAND

Siberia

JAPAN

SOUTH KOREA

UNION OF SOVIET SOCIALIST REPUBLICS
(SOVIET UNION)

CHINA

VIETNAM

PHILIPPINES

THAILAND

INDONESIA

AUSTRALIA

INDIA

BANGLADESH

PAKISTAN

IRAN

SAUDI
ARABIA

INDIAN
OCEAN

90° E

TURKEY

ISRAEL

EGYPT

ETHIOPIA

SOUTH AFRICA

ZAIRE

Antarctica

WEST
GERMANY

GREAT
BRITAIN

FRANCE

SPAIN

ITALY

NIGERIA

0°

IRELAND

LIBERIA

Greenland

ATLANTIC
OCEAN

BRAZIL

ARGENTINA

CANADA

UNITED
STATES

CUBA

PERU

90° W

90° W

UNITED STATES

CANADA

MEXICO

Equator

Alaska

Hawaii

PACIFIC OCEAN

NEW ZEALAND

180°

JAPAN

SOUTH KOREA

PHILIPPINES

VIETNAM

THAILAND

INDONESIA

AUSTRALIA

Siberia

ARCTIC OCEAN

UNION OF SOVIET SOCIALIST REPUBLICS
(SOVIET UNION)

CHINA

INDIA

BANGLADESH

PAKISTAN

IRAN

90° E

INDIAN OCEAN

Antarctica

SAUDI ARABIA

TURKEY

ISRAEL

ETHIOPIA

EGYPT

WEST GERMANY

ITALY

SPAIN

FRANCE

GREAT BRITAIN

IRELAND

NIGERIA

ZAIRE

SOUTH AFRICA

LIBERIA

0°

Greenland

ATLANTIC OCEAN

BRAZIL

ARGENTINA

PERU

CANADA

UNITED STATES

CUBA

90° W

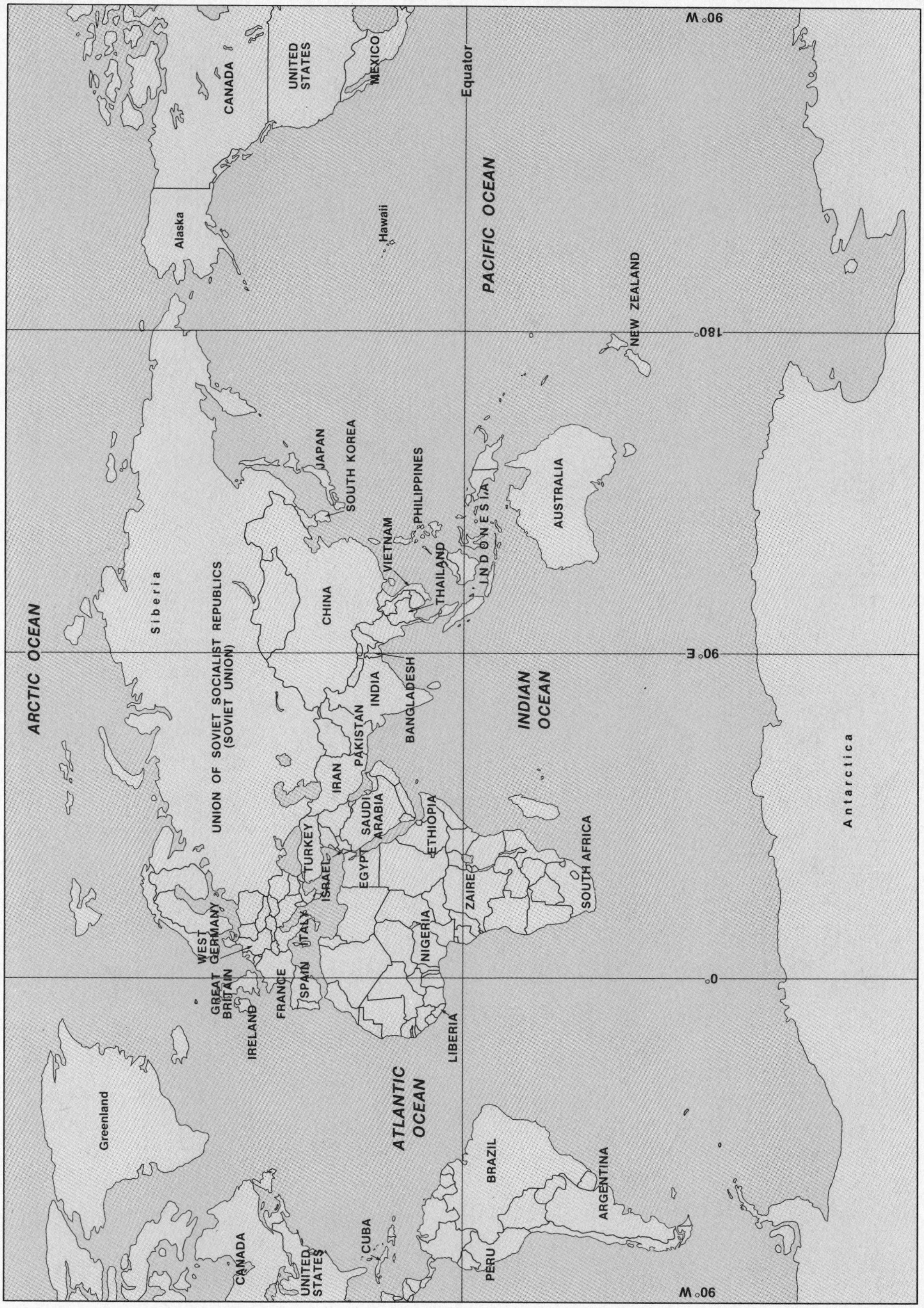
ARCTIC OCEAN
Greenland
CANADA
UNITED STATES
CUBA
PERU
BRAZIL
ARGENTINA
ATLANTIC OCEAN
IRELAND
GREAT BRITAIN
FRANCE
SPAIN
WEST GERMANY
ITALY
LIBERIA
NIGERIA
ZAIRE
SOUTH AFRICA
ISRAEL
EGYPT
TURKEY
SAUDI ARABIA
ETHIOPIA
IRAN
PAKISTAN
INDIA
BANGLADESH
UNION OF SOVIET SOCIALIST REPUBLICS
(SOVIET UNION)
Siberia
CHINA
VIETNAM
THAILAND
INDONESIA
PHILIPPINES
SOUTH KOREA
JAPAN
AUSTRALIA
INDIAN OCEAN
Antarctica
NEW ZEALAND
PACIFIC OCEAN
Hawaii
Alaska
CANADA
UNITED STATES
MEXICO
Equator
90° W
0°
90° E
180°
90° W

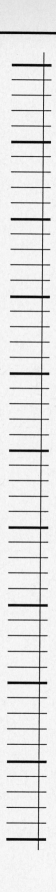

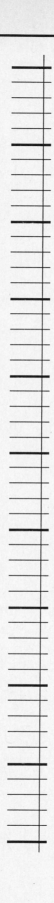

MAPPING AMERICAN HISTORY CORRELATIONS

CORRELATIONS WITH DIVINE 2/E (1991)

Chapter	Source Maps	Useful Reference Maps	Map Lessons
Introduction	1–2, 60	1–5, 50	1–6
1	1–3, 10–12	7, 21	7
2	47	8, 21, 24	9, 12
3	7, 9	6, 8, 24	8, 10, 12
4	8–10	6, 8, 25	8, 10, 12
5	13–15	8, 26	11, 12
6	16–17	21–23	18
7	17–18	6, 8, 43	13, 18
8	18–21	1, 27, 43	14, 18
9	22–24, 27	17, 25–27, 33	14, 18
10	24–27	17, 33	15, 18
11	30–33	33, 44	16, 18
12	34, 36	1, 9, 17, 28	14, 15
13	37, 39	31–32, 37	18
14	34, 39	9, 22–23	18
15	40–42	37, 45–46	17
16	43–45	19, 34	19, 24
17	36, 49	7, 17, 19, 23	24
18	46–48, 58	34, 40, 46–47	20, 24
19	46–48, 52, 54, 58	34, 35	20, 21, 22
20	52–55	5, 10, 11	24
21	56–57, 59	50	24
22	54, 58–63	18, 21–22	21, 24
23	54, 56, 58–59	18, 35	21, 23
24	57, 64–66	50	23, 24
25	64, 67–69	35, 41, 48	23, 25, 30
26	70–72	12, 31–32, 48	26, 30
27	71–75	50	27–28
28	76–78	50	30
29	78–82	13, 23, 42, 49	30
30	78, 87	50	30
31	85	14–16, 32–32	29
32	82–84	22–23, 49–50	31–32
33	86–90	22–23, 31–32, 49–50	33–34

CORRELATIONS WITH GARRATY 7/E (1991)

Chapter	Source Maps	Useful Reference Maps	Map Lessons
Introduction	1–2, 60	1–5, 50	1–6
1	1–7	7–8, 24	7–9, 12
2	7–9	8, 21, 24	10
3	9–12	6, 8, 24–25, 50	12
4	13–16	8, 26	11
5	16–18	4, 6, 8, 43	13
6	19–21	1, 8, 27, 43	14
7	22–24	17, 26, 27, 33	14, 18
8	23, 24, 27	3–5, 33	14, 18
9	24, 27, 29, 37	33, 44	14, 18
10	24–29	17, 18, 28, 30	18

Chapter	Source Maps	Useful Reference Maps	Map Lessons
11	27–33	9, 18, 44	15, 16
12	24, 27, 35	9, 21	18
13	34–39	5, 28, 30, 44	15, 16
14	30, 35, 38	9, 17–18, 44–45	14–16
15	34, 37, 39	1, 5, 9, 22, 37, 40	17–18
16	40–42	37, 45–46	17
17	43–45	19, 34	19
18	43–45	6, 10, 11, 17, 19	19, 24
19	58	23, 34, 46–47	19, 20
20	46–51	10–11, 18, 21, 34	20, 22
21	49, 52, 58	21, 22	24
22	53, 55, 56	11, 23, 31–32, 47	20, 22, 24
23	55–57	29, 50	21, 24
24	54, 58–63	18, 21–22	24, 25
25	64–66	35, 50	23, 24
26	67–69, 71	35, 41, 48	23, 25, 26
27	67–69, 70	35, 38, 41, 48	25, 26
28	70–73	12, 21–23, 31–32, 48	25, 26
29	73–75	49, 50	27–28
30	76–79	36, 49	30
31	80–85	15–16, 20, 23, 31–32	11, 35
32	89, 90	15–16, 49	31, 32, 34
33	85–90	23, 31–32, 39, 42, 50	33, 35

CORRELATIONS WITH NASH 2/E (1990) AND NASH, BRIEF (1992)

Chapter	Source Maps	Useful Reference Maps	Map Lessons
Introduction	1–2, 60	1–5, 50	1–6
1	1–3	1–7, 50	7, 12
2	3–7	1–8, 24, 50	8–9, 12
3	7–10	1–8, 24, 50	9–10, 12
4	7–10	8, 21	8, 10, 12
5	9–13	24–26, 50	11, 12
6	13–15	8, 25	11, 18
7	16–17	22, 25	18
8	16–19	8, 25	13, 18
9	19–24	8, 17	14, 18
10	19–24	27, 33, 43	15–16, 18
11	23–29	9, 18, 21–23	15–16, 18
12	30, 37	15, 21–23	15, 18
13	31–33	21–23	18
14	31–33, 35–36	1–6, 9–10	14, 18
15	37–39	28, 30	14, 18
16	40–42	9, 30, 37, 40, 45–46	17, 18
17	43–44, 64	19, 29, 34	19, 24
18	35, 53–56	37–38, 46	16, 24
19	45–48	11, 23, 34, 40–41	20–24
20	49–51	18, 20, 31	20–24
21	55–57	50	1–2, 24
22	52–54, 58–63	18–20, 47	20–24
23	64–66	35, 38, 41, 48	1–2, 24
24	64–69	35, 38, 41, 48	25, 30
25	70–72	12, 31–32, 48	25, 26, 30
26	73–75	18, 50	27–28, 30
27	76–78	36, 49–50	29–30
28	79–84	36, 39, 42, 49	31, 35
29	85–87	31–32, 36, 50	31, 32, 35
30	85, 88	13–16	33–35
31	86–90	22–23, 49–50	33–35